AGGRESSION: Our Asian Disaster

aggression:

OUR ASIAN DISASTER

William L. Standard

Random House: New York

 Published in the United States by Random House, Inc., New York, and simultaneously in Canada by Random House of Canada Limited, Toronto.

ISBN: 0–394–47080–x

Library of Congress Catalog Card Number: 76–143829

Manufactured in the United States of America by Kingsport Press
98765432

First Edition

To
Samuel David Standard

INTRODUCTION

by Wayne Morse

William L. Standard presents a keen, factual analysis of United States aggression in Vietnam. He writes about our outlawry as it was from the beginning and continues to be. We are a proud people, as we should be, because there is so much in our history of which to be very proud. Therefore, it is difficult for Americans to face up to the ugly realities of our military and diplomatic wrongdoings in Southeast Asia.

The author not only indicts our country as a military aggressor in Southeast Asia, but documents his conclusions as to our violations of constitutional and international law. To select one chapter for special commendation is somewhat unfair because it might seem to de-emphasize the significance of the other topics in Mr. Standard's analysis of our government's mistakes in Southeast Asia. Nevertheless, Chapter V, entitled "United States Intervention in Vietnam is Illegal," does deserve special stress. It is an unanswerable rebuttal to those who say, "It doesn't make any difference now about the mistakes we might have made in going into Vietnam. The fact is that we are in, and now we must see it through." Of course, the mistakes we made in getting into the war make a great deal of difference, because we as a nation must recognize and rectify them if we are to have any hope of reaching an agreement for an honorable peace settlement.

Most of the people of the world know of our military aggression in Vietnam. Unfortunately, too many of our own citizens still do not know of it, or cannot bring themselves to admit it. Too many Americans appear to think that we can finally force a surrender to our military might by more killing, more devastation, more escalation of our war brutality upon a people without a navy, without an air force, without comparable fire power, without matchable military training, without unlimited economic resources. They seem deaf to the verdict of world public opinion as shown by the fact that not a single major nation supports our record of inhumanity in Vietnam.

Chapter V, in discussing the illegality of the war with respect both to our own Constitution and to international law, shows how important it is that our nation bring its foreign policy back inside the framework of the Constitution and of our international-law treaty obligations. We must return to practicing the ideal that we have taught our young for decades: that the substitution of the Rule of Law for the Jungle Law of military might is mankind's only hope for permanent peace. There is no hope for peace unless the nations of the world who have signed such treaties as the United Nations Charter will honor their signatures and will jointly enforce the peace wherever and whenever it is threatened. The peace keeping procedures of the United Nations, and other treaties subject to the controlling jurisdiction of the United Nations, offer at the present stage of the development of international law the best hope of avoiding a nuclear holocaust from which no nation will survive as a victor.

The other chapters amply support an ugly reality which the American people must confront before it is too late: that the Eisenhower-Nixon-Dulles military containment policy of 1953 was the incubator which hatched our ultimate aggression in Vietnam. Richard Nixon, as President, has given no indication of rejecting that doctrine. On the contrary, when he promised in Bangkok, on his Asian trip, that the United States would come to Thailand's defense if she should be attacked from without, he restated the military containment policy for Asia to which he was a party in 1953.

By what right did he pledge the lives of countless American youths as though they were his Presidential pawns to be played on an international military chessboard? The sad fact is that President Nixon has made no pledge to the American people to get out of Asia militarily. His promise to withdraw troops from Vietnam deserves approval, but it calls for the American people to ask when and how many. We need to ask, also, how many will remain in Vietnam for five, ten, twenty years, or longer. What agreements has President Nixon made with Thieu and Ky about withdrawal of American troops? What about Thailand, Laos, and Burma? What about any other secret commitments involving the use of American troops?

This book is further proof that it is important for the American people to insist that Congress recapture the Constitutional checks upon the military practices that Presidents have come to exercise outside of their Constitutional powers with respect to committing the United States to war.

Eugene, Oregon
November 15, 1969

CONTENTS

AGGRESSION: Our Asian Disaster

1:

The New Colonialism

The United States has been involved in Vietnam for more than twenty years. For more than four years American troops have been fighting in Vietnam, with losses of almost 45,000 in dead and about 300,000 in nonfatal casualties.[1] Billions of dollars have been expended for a cause that in no way involves American security.

The aim of this book is to show how we became involved in Vietnam, why our presence there is illegal and constitutes an act of aggression, and why the war in Vietnam may be endless. By examining this dark chapter in the world's legal and moral history, we may hope to find a way of ending this war and preventing future similar aggressions.

According to one well-informed political analyst, "The American people have lost stomach for the war in Vietnam." In 1969 students at American colleges declared, in petitions to President Nixon and at graduating exercises, that "if confronted with the draft, they would refuse induction, thereby risking jail sentences and jeopardizing careers to oppose the war."

If, during the coming year, the draftees from all walks of life should emulate the college graduates in their preference for "jail sentences" to service in the Vietnam war, then

America will be faced with the possibility of losing its first war. But what is more important, we may lose our standing as *"the* great" power and the shining example of "freedom and justice for all" throughout the world.

The war in Vietnam can be terminated only by a total withdrawal of U.S. combat forces from Vietnam. The American people could then make a new commitment to the Vietnamese people, which would appropriately be a resolution to at least make restitution for the devastation of these years of war.

Remembering that those who do not understand history are doomed to repeat it, we might profitably make a further resolution: to learn the lessons of Vietnam so well that we will never again find ourselves as a nation waging illegal and unjust wars to protect American investments in economic and military vacuums left by former empires.

There are not enough human lives in the United States to make such wars successful; nor, it will soon be discovered, is there enough money in America to make them successful. Most of us in America still believe that we can regain our morality as a nation, and that when we do, we will not feel called upon to try to replace England, France, or the other nineteenth-century colonial empires anywhere in the world.

Unless the American people and the peoples of the world recognize these facts, peace will not come to the world in the nuclear age.

President Dwight D. Eisenhower, in the closing days of his administration, warned his country against the "military-industrial complex" and stated that the security of America was threatened by the unrestrained ambitions of this sector of the American people. Ending the war in Vietnam is the vital next step toward world peace, but that alone will not

~~Higgins 65~~ Standard 1971
aggressive impreciation

96	STATUS: EXPIRED	UPDATED	CIGARS	
02	STATUS: CURRENT	UPDATED 01/10/200	CIGARS	
03	STATUS: CURRENT	UPDATED 01/28/200	CIGARS	
01	STATUS: EXPIRED	UPDATED 05/12/200	CIGARS	
03	STATUS: CURRENT	UPDATED 03/07/200	CIGARS	
	STATUS: MAIL	UPDATED	CIGARS	
02	STATUS: EXPIRED	UPDATED 07/05/200	CIGARS	
97	STATUS: EXPIRED	UPDATED	CIGARS	
02	STATUS: CURRENT	UPDATED 11/02/200	CIGARS	
98	STATUS: EXPIRED	UPDATED	CIGARS	
02	STATUS: EXPIRED	UPDATED 07/05/200	CIGARS	
00	STATUS: EXPIRED	UPDATED 07/22/199	CIGARS	
97	STATUS: EXPIRED	UPDATED	782	
01	STATUS: EXPIRED	UPDATED 01/13/200	CIGARS	
97	STATUS: EXPIRED	UPDATED	CIGARS	

necessarily bring peace to the world. In truth, the military-industrial complex has been frighteningly strengthened by the war, as well as by the careful nurturing by the Nixon administration.

With the Cambodian invasion and the literal obliteration of Laos, the involvement of Thailand and Indonesia is only a matter of time. Neither the Filipinos nor the Australians nor the new Zealanders are militarily or economically strong enough to withstand the holocaust which will take place in that part of the world if conventional weapons are replaced by nuclear warheads supplied by the nuclear powers. And if nuclear war in any form whatsoever comes to any part of the world, whether defenses against it are established in "thin" or "thick" forms, humanity will be extinguished.

When the United Nations was established, many people hoped an international form of coexistence had been created that would be strong enough to prevent any nation from unilaterally making war. Our unilateral involvement in Vietnam is an ugly demonstration of American contempt of humanity's desire for peace, as well as evidence of the tragic lack of unity among the nuclear nations. The United Nations Charter was the first attempt at administration of world coexistence, because the veto power of the Security Council makes it quite clear that if peace is to be maintained in the world, there must be unity between the great powers. That unity, regrettably, does not exist—indeed, one of the great powers, China, is routinely excluded from the United Nations in each year's Assembly vote. Nor are we to assume that the NATO Alliance or the Warsaw Pact or any other "regional security" treaty is a guarantee of peace. If humanity is to survive, peace-loving people and organizations in every single country throughout the world must unite to confront the world military-industrial complex and say, "We will not die for economic expansion and domination of one people by another."

The massive world-wide demonstrations of 1969 and 1970 show that the demand for peace is increasing in intensity. Escalating dissent is of special importance in the United States, which, as the center of the world military-industrial complex, is in this decade both the richest and the most overtly aggressive country in the world.

2:

The Escalation of Resistance

A. Dissension at Home

The graduating classes of 1969 listened to the valedictory addresses and laid aside their caps and gowns. They now awaited induction into the Army for service in Vietnam.

In the fall of 1964 the members of these classes were high school seniors, starry-eyed and full of idealism, looking forward to the next stage of their academic lives.

The 1964 presidential campaign oratory commanded the attention of some of them. On August 12, 1964, President Johnson, addressing a New York audience, stated:

> Some others are eager to enlarge the conflict. They call upon us to supply American boys to do the job that Asian boys should do. They ask us to take reckless action which might risk the lives of millions and engulf much of Asia and certainly threaten the peace of the entire world. Moreover, such action would offer no solution at all to the real problem of Vietnam.

As the campaign grew warmer, he spoke up directly on the subject of bombing North Vietnam, and on August 29, 1964, he declared in Texas:

> I have had advice to lead our planes with bombs and to drop them on certain areas that I think would enlarge the war and escalate the war, and result in our committing a good many American boys to fighting a war that I think ought to be fought by the boys of Asia to help protect their own land. And for that reason, I haven't chosen to enlarge the war.

His final statement in this vein was made on September 28, 1964, when he addressed a Manchester, New Hampshire, audience:

> So we are not going North and we are not going South; we are going to continue to try to get them to save their own freedom with their own men, with our leadership and our officer direction, and such equipment as we can furnish them. We think that losing 190 lives in the period that we have been out there is bad. But it is not like 190,000 that we might lose the first month if we escalated that war. So we are trying somehow to evolve a way, as we have in some other places, where the North Vietnamese and the Chinese Communists finally, after getting worn down, conclude that they will leave their neighbors alone. And if they do, we will come home tomorrow.

Before President Johnson made these speeches, however, he had already procured the adoption of the Tonkin Bay Resolution. According to its senatorial supporters, the resolution was intended to grant the President power to meet the situation of an attack upon American vessels in the Tonkin Bay area.

Our high school seniors, of course, knew nothing about the implications that resolution had for them. Not even Congress foresaw that President Johnson would rely upon it to dispense with the declaration of war that is required by the United States Constitution, when he ordered the bombing of North Vietnam on February 7, 1965. America had enjoyed comparative peace since 1954, when the Korean war came to an end. To most of those who were to become members of the Class of 1969, the Korean war and World War II were nothing more than a few pages in a history assignment.

The fall-winter semesters in the high schools and colleges were tranquil. President Johnson's campaign assurances, however, were soon enough dissipated. Less than a month after his inauguration, North Vietnam was bombed and America was launched on a war ten thousand miles from home.

Fanned by such broken promises and false rhetoric, the era of *campus protests* began and spread out of control. The revolt at the University of California at Berkeley in 1964 was essentially rooted in the students' resentment of what they considered bureaucratic practices identified with the political right. But as student rebellions spread to Columbia, Wisconsin, San Francisco State, Harvard, Duke, Cornell, Brandeis, the issues were not limited to matters of curriculum, the role of students in administration, and the status of blacks and other minority groups on the campus. In most of the revolts of 1967 and 1968, opposition to the recruiting of the Dow Chemical Company, to army recruiting, and to the role of the R.O.T.C. showed the students' basic opposition to American involvement in the Vietnam war.

Revolts at American colleges were by no means unknown. One historian reports six rebellions at Princeton between 1800 and 1830. In one case the students at Lane Seminary in Ohio walked out en masse over the slavery issue and moved to the more congenial surroundings of Oberlin, whose students were actively assisting runaway slaves to reach freedom.[1] During the twentieth century, however, political rebellion among college youth has been so rare that the current wave of revolt seems to mystify the majority of the American public.

After the disturbances at Columbia University in April and May of 1968, a fact-finding commission was appointed to investigate the causes of such violence. Archibald Cox, Professor of Law at Harvard University, was chairman of the commission. Excerpts from the commission's reports are indeed revealing. The overall opinion of the commission was that "the present generation of young people in our universities is the best informed, the most intelligent and the most idealistic this country has ever known. This is the experience of teachers everywhere."

The attitudes and concerns of the students are poignantly disclosed in these findings.

> During the years in which the present university students were in secondary school, the gap between the generations was evidenced by the marked changes in speech, conduct, dress and manners. . . .
>
> As one student observed during our investigation, today's students take seriously the ideals taught in schools and churches, and often at home, and then they see a system that denies its ideals in its actual life. Racial injustice and the war in Vietnam stand out as prime illustrations of our society's deviation from its professed ideals and the slowness with which the system reforms itself.

The Columbia University commission concluded that, while the students' opinions covered the entire spectrum of political life, "two issues command unusually broad agreement among the young and engage their deepest emotions: the peace movement and racial justice. Both were causes of the April disturbances." [2]

The student revolt at Columbia was perhaps the most demonstrative manifestation of rebellion, but insurgency also began to appear on more restrained campuses.

The July 20, 1968, issue of *The New Yorker* magazine carried an article entitled "College Seniors and the War," which reported that at Dartmouth College (one of the most conservative colleges in New England, with a student body composed largely of very solid members of the upper middle class), the graduating class heard its valedictorian urge his classmates to refuse to be drafted and to refuse to fight and to go to Canada. According to the author of the article, the valedictorian of 1968 did not speak for a majority of the senior class, but the class had taken its own poll on the war that spring, getting opinions from about 530 members. Hardly any enthusiasm for the war appeared. The class found that about 65 percent of its members were for an immediate withdrawal, without any delay for negotiations.

Resistance to the war increased. In April of 1969, 253 student leaders and campus editors presented a statement to President Nixon vowing that they would go to jail rather than join the armed forces as long as the war in Vietnam continued. The signers of this statement were students from such leading universities as Harvard, Yale, Princeton, Columbia, Cornell, Stanford, the University of Wisconsin, the University of Michigan, the University of California, and New York University.

The students' statement concluded: "Along with thousands of our fellow students, we campus leaders cannot participate in a war which we consider to be immoral and unjust. We will not serve in the military as long as the war in Vietnam continues." [3]

The *New York Times* in an editorial on June 23, 1969,

commented on the conduct of these students, saying that they vigorously oppose being forced to fight against their consciences in a war in Vietnam that they regard as unnecessary, immoral, and unjust. These men are not, by and large, cowards or slackers, as some superficially contend. Many of them would be among the first to volunteer for duty in time of real national need.

In addition to those who signed the statement to President Nixon, most of whom were college seniors or graduate students facing the prospect of being drafted in the weeks or months after they finished school, there are today many American deserters and exiles who have sought asylum in Sweden, Canada, and elsewhere.

The extent to which the actions of war resisters are being acknowledged as permissible is shown in a statement by Allan J. MacEachen, Minister of Immigration, who announced that the Canadian Government had decided to allow U.S. military deserters to enter Canada and, unless otherwise ineligible, to let them stay. MacEachen indicated that the admission of resisters had never been challenged in Canada. The basic position of the Canadian Government is that "the question of an individual's membership or potential membership in the armed services of his own country is a matter to be settled between the individual and his government and is not a matter in which we should become involved." [4]

It is interesting to note that since this chapter was begun, several states (among others, Massachusetts, Pennsylvania, Illinois, and Rhode Island) have introduced bills in their state legislatures designed to protect, under law, any resident of a state, inducted or serving in the military forces of the United States, from service in an undeclared war outside of the territorial limits of the United States. More explicitly, what is being tested is the President's power to act without the official sanction and declaration by that body of government to which the power to declare war has been granted under the Constitution—namely, the Congress.*

In the case of New York State, a law already exists which provides such protection for the residents of that state. Section 5 in the Declaration of Rights in the New York Bill of Rights of 1787 and in the Revised Laws of 1813 states that "no citizen of this state can be constrained to arm himself, or to go out of this state, or to find soldiers or men of arms, either horsemen or footmen, without the grant and assent of the people of this state, by their representatives in senate and assembly except in the cases specially provided for by the Constitution of the United States." [5]

Senator J. William Fulbright, appearing on a national television broadcast, *Face the Nation,* made the following observation:

> I am sure in my own mind that Vietnam is probably the principal cause in the background of the student riots. And nothing distresses me more than what is happening to our younger generation. I get an awful lot of letters. I have had several this week from both students who were here, and I have had them from people, young men, and you obviously see from their letters, the most sensitive class of our young men who have left this country. There have been a lot of them, you know. I think some 50,000 have emigrated from this country to other countries because of their disillusionment with what their country is doing. And they are among the best. I had a most impressive letter from a man in one of the colleges the other day, making this point in a way I

* The Constitution of the United States, Article I, Section 8, Clause 11.

> can't possibly make here as to the best, the most sensitive, intelligent students are the ones who are most alienated; the raw material for the brownshirts are staying in there, you know, and they're not leaving. They like it and they are going to stay and they may set the tone for the next generation.[6]

A teaching fellow in sociology at Harvard University, in a letter to the *New York Times* about the occupation of University Hall by students, wrote:

> We did not risk policemen's clubs and expulsion from school to eliminate just any example of unjustified privilege at Harvard. We wanted to abolish R.O.T.C. because of what it does, and especially because of its contribution to the brutal war in Vietnam, where thousands of men, women and children are dying while President Nixon looks for a face-saving way to give up.[7]

It is not only college students who have evidenced unrest over Vietnam. A recent study of *protests and disruptions by students in high schools and junior high schools* has been conducted by Professor Alan F. Westin, Director of the Center for Research and Education in American Liberties at Columbia University. Dr. Westin's study was based on the monitoring of 1,800 daily newspapers. As reported in the *New York Times* of May 9, 1969, Dr. Westin classified 361 disruptive high school cases as follows: *

---

* Although the classification of disruptive cases places racial and political protests in two separate categories, it is interesting to bear in mind the fact that the involvement in Vietnam of a disproportionate number of blacks (to the overall proportion of blacks in the general population) would tend to indicate that these two categories are not mutually exclusive.

TYPE OF PROTEST	NUMBER OF INCIDENTS	STATES INVOLVED
Racial	132	27
Political (including Vietnam)	81	21
Against dress regulations	71	25
Against discipline	60	28
For educational reforms	17	14

In addition to its revelation of appalling racial tension, what is of particular interest here is the large number of incidents that centered on political questions, "including Vietnam."

Although there are many Americans who would like to discredit all protest against the war as the work of a small and extreme minority, there is considerable evidence that our aggression in Vietnam is also attracting a growing audience, willing to speak their mind and act on their words, at the *grass-roots level.*

Growing concern about the meaning of the sacrifices demanded of American families is symbolized in a news story about the mother of a slain G.I. who returned the medals awarded to her son, an Army lieutenant who died in Vietnam on May 11, 1968. Mrs. Louise B. Ransom, when returning the medals to the counselor of the South Vietnam Embassy, stated that her twenty-two-year-old son Robert had died "for a government which its own people do not want." Mrs. Ransom added that the South Vietnamese Government was "suppressing the freedom of the South Vietnamese people." [8]

The *New York Times* of May 2, 1969, published a report from the rural community of Beallsville, Ohio, whose City Council decided to erect a flagpole and a granite plaque in the town cemetery, where four of Beallsville's Vietnam dead were buried. The town of Beallsville has a population of 450. Six of its young men have been killed in the past three years—about ninety times the national average. Ben F. Gramlich, the mayor, whose own son is still in Vietnam, observed:

> We'd like to do something else to try to get the boys home and to keep others from trying to go, but we don't know what to do. . . . We are going to put the flagpole and the plaque up here, where the plaque can be seen from both of these roads.

The attitude of the 1969 graduating class was demonstrated at commencement exercises throughout the country.* At Hunter College, in New York City, where 1,100 baccalaureate degrees and 525 masters degrees were awarded, the keynote addresses all demanded the immediate termination of the war in Vietnam. "Some of the faculty members and graduates wore armbands proclaiming their opposition to the draft." [9]

At the 201st commencement at Brown University, Dr. Henry A. Kissinger, President Nixon's National Security Assistant, was awarded an honorary degree. About two-thirds of the 900 graduating seniors turned their backs when Dr. Kissinger received his degree. A statement signed by the class read, "Dr. Kissinger is a symbol of the war effort in Vietnam. This war is senseless and immoral." [10]

Yale University has a tradition under which there are no speeches in the commencement program, and the awarding of degrees is emphasized. The Yale commencement of June 1969 broke that tradition. The first student to speak

---

* In a subsequent chapter (Chapter Eleven), we deal more fully with the "ferment on the campus" in the spring and summer of 1970.

at a Yale University commencement since 1894 told 12,000 graduates and faculty members that "frustration and despair" overwhelmed the senior class because of the war in Vietnam.

William McIlwaine Thompson, Jr., a Virginian who was the senior class secretary, the highest elective office of a Yale class, said: "We are told that the pride of the nation is at stake. Pride is expendable; lives are not. Within the next year some of us will die, others will be maimed, in a war which has been declared a mistake. And yet it continues."

In his brief remarks, Thompson also stated that 731 seniors, or 77 percent of the class, had recently signed a petition urging that their commencement express opposition to the war. He said:

> In addition, 143 members of the class signed a petition indicating that if confronted with the draft they would refuse induction, thereby risking jail sentences and jeopardizing careers to oppose the war.
>
> And finally, a majority of the class has pledged to contribute to a legal defense fund established to help with the legal fees of those members of the class refusing induction. . . .
>
> The war is destroying not one nation but two—the Vietnamese and our own. Our cities are in decay; our universities are in chaos; our poor are hungry.
>
> And yet our money and our energies are expended upon war and the perpetuation of war. . . .
>
> For the past four years our leaders have attempted to soothe us with predictions of peace. We are tired of their rhetoric—of promises to act without action; of a willingness to take risks without risks. False rhetoric is no longer acceptable. . . .
>
> We will not be appeased by cynical attempts to silence public criticism of the war.[11]

B. The Provocation for Protest

While the Vietnam war has had an overwhelming and ever-increasing effect upon the conscience of the American people, it must still be borne in mind that the full force of the United States effort in Vietnam is measured in altogether different terms in Vietnam itself. It would be safe to assume that the majority of the American public is made aware of only a fraction of the devastation and death which the Vietnamese people suffer daily. However, the pendulum is swinging, and although primary sources are still few and far between, the American people are slowly beginning to understand, and to some extent feel, the frustration, anxiety, desperation, and death of a country halfway around the world.

The extent to which the American people have lost stomach for the war is in no small measure governed by the reports from the Vietnam battlefront.

The intensity of the bombing of North Vietnam in the spring of 1965, as well as the bombardment of South Vietnam, soon revealed the military's disregard of the conventions governing the conduct of war, and forced many Americans to become deeply concerned at the wantonness with which the war was being carried on. It appeared to them that during the first years of the war the American General Staff was determined to wage a war of a *Schrecklichkeit* * type, in the hope that this method of warfare would terrorize the Vietnamese people and bring about an early surrender.

---

* Ger. "frightfulness, horror."

In 1965 and 1966 the American conduct of the war became characterized by consistent violations of almost every international agreement relating to the rules of warfare, and it has continued in this pattern.

An organization called Clergy and Laymen Concerned About Vietnam invited Professor Seymour Melman of Columbia University to do an in-depth study into the dispatches about the war which were carried in newspapers and magazines, as well as treatises. Professor Melman and his research associates completed what proved to be a monumental achievement. Their study, *In the Name of America,* was published by Clergy and Laymen Concerned about Vietnam in January of 1968. The dispatches quoted cover the years 1965 to 1967 inclusive.

The clergy and laymen who commissioned the book were mindful of the fact that the reports themselves would make difficult as well as distressing reading. They therefore prepared a commentary on the contents of the book, a "Perspective for Readers," to serve as an introduction. This commentary was signed by thirty clergymen, including deans of divinity schools and scholars at theological seminaries, as well as lay people.

Four paragraphs of the commentary are especially significant:

> The news dispatches that follow do not make pleasant reading. Their cumulative effect is overpowering, for they do not merely confirm what we all know, that the war in Vietnam is dirty and inhumane, but they also establish something few of us have known, that American conduct in Vietnam has been characterized by consistent violation of almost every international agreement relating to the rules of warfare. . . . (Introduction, p. 1.)
>
> Another disturbing matter raised by the dispatches cen-

ters on the racial dimension of the war. We need to ask ourselves whether it is likely that our nation, or our soldiers, would give moral consent to the things we are doing in Vietnam if they were being done against white people. The demeaning term "gooks" and the use of such language as "skunk hunting" to describe shooting at Vietnamese from low-flying planes are only symbols of the problem. We were morally shocked when the Germans destroyed the entire village of Lidice in Czechoslovakia, and when a "scorched earth" policy became routine for the Nazi armies. And yet we are not shocked at the total destruction of South Vietnamese villages. Would we find ourselves passively consenting to such atrocities if they were being committed against the French or the Irish or the Danes? The destruction of a Vietnamese "hut" appears to us a minor matter; would we feel the same way if it were the croft of a highland Scot or the home of a Dutch banker? (pp. 9–10.)

The distinction between combatants and noncombatants, military and civilian personnel, is an ancient one. All the treaties and conventions on laws of warfare make clear that specific measures must be taken to minimize civilian casualties, and that particular precautions must be taken to avoid them whenever possible. But in almost all military operations in Vietnam it is clear in advance that civilians will be inevitable casualties. For example, one of our most "ordinary" military operations, pattern bombing from high altitudes, is completely indiscriminate; any persons within a given area, whether military or civilian, guerrillas or children, young soldiers or aged civilians, are likely to be wounded or killed. Not only do bombs dropped from our B-52s fail to discriminate between military and civilian personnel, but the strafing of villages from low-flying planes is similarly impartial in failing to distinguish combatants from noncombatants. When sampans are bombed or strafed, the bombs and the bullets tear the flesh of civilians just as cruelly as the flesh of military. Our naval bombardment of coastal villages, often situated in areas where no

> battle is being waged, is similarly indiscriminate. Even when we concentrate on villages assumed to have a high percentage of Viet Cong leaders, or to be headquarters for Viet Cong activities, such information is sometimes inaccurate, and the dispatches indicate a high number of "mistakes," in which we have bombed, strafed or napalmed "friendly" villages, thus driving the civilian toll even higher. (pp. 5–6.)
>
> Individuals may be strafed from the air. They may be shot at with M-16 rifles whose bullets not only enter the human body but expand upon doing so, causing needless and excruciating pain far beyond that necessary to incapacitate the victim. They may have napalm or white phosphorus bombs dropped on them. Napalm, a jelly-like gasoline, clings to the skin and cannot be scraped off, burning and melting human flesh, while white phosphorus continues to burn even within the human body. Napalm sucks up all the oxygen in confined areas so that those who escape being burned to death will suffocate for lack of air. Fragmentation weapons are cannisters containing hundreds of pellets or pieces of sharp metal; when they explode the pellets lodge deep in the bodies of all within range. These can be timed to go off at intervals, so that long after an air raid civilians returning to their villages or fields may be cruelly wounded by the chunks of flying metal. (p. 6.)

The areas of special concern for Professor Melman and his collaborators were the treatment of prisoners, the indiscriminate killing of civilians, and the hardships to which civilians are exposed. The fifteen chapters of *In the Name of America* address themselves to, among other topics, the illegal treatment, illegal interrogation, terror, mutilation and, at times, murder of prisoners of war, as well as the wounded in the field; the unwarranted use of gas; and the destruction of huts and villages in the fulfillment of a "scorched earth" policy.

Some chapters are devoted to aerial bombardments of

areas described as "free bomb zones," where an unrestrained pattern of bombardment described as "pattern bombing" was directed essentially at the harassment and collective punishment of civilians in "concentrated target areas." And finally, chapters are devoted to the capricious destruction and defoliation of target areas.

The revolts on the campuses and the growing resistance to the Vietnam war can be fully understood only if we are aware of such aspects of our involvement. For that reason we must devote a few pages to excerpts from the book itself. With the permission of Clergy and Laymen Concerned About Vietnam, the following is quoted from *In the Name of America:*

Prisoners of War and the Wounded in the Field

> Under *The Hague Convention of 1907, Article 4:*
> Prisoners of war are in the power of the hostile government, but not of the individuals or corps who capture them. They must be humanely treated. . . . (p. 29.)
>
> Under *The Geneva Convention of 1949, Article 12:*
> Prisoners of war are in the hands of the enemy Power, but not of the individuals or military units who have captured them. Irrespective of the individual responsibilities that may exist, the Detaining Power is responsible for the treatment given them. (p. 56.)
>
> 29 Nov. 65 *Newsweek.*
> . . . Some of the American wounded, caught by the enemy, had apparently been given the *coup de grace* with a bullet in the head. "They were not interested in taking prisoners," said McTigue grimly. But neither were some of the Americans. In one place, the GIs came upon three wounded North Vietnamese. One lay huddled under a tree, a smile on his face. "You won't smile anymore," snapped one of the soldiers, pumping bullets into his body. The other two met the same fate. (p. 60.)

Dec. 65 *Ramparts:* Bernard Fall, "This isn't Munich. It's Spain."

. . . In this war, there is no respect for the wounded. The Communist prisoner in the photograph had been shot in the back. He was bleeding when I found him lying on the floor in a Vietnamese Command Post. A journalist from a New York paper came in and asked to photograph him. The South Vietnamese officer in the room raised the wounded man matter-of-factly and propped him against a table leg for the photographer. The prisoner grimaced in pain.

I told an American officer who was with the unit that the man was wounded and should get some attention. His answer: "Yes, I know he needs help, but there isn't anything I can do about it. He's in Vietnamese hands. That is why I walked away, don't you see?" I saw. I also walked away and said nothing. (p. 61.)

21 Jul. 66 *St. Louis Post-Dispatch,* Washington, July 20.

Sen. Stephen M. Young, D-Ohio, said today the South Vietnamese are executing many prisoners of war turned over to them by American fighting forces. Young said that "in the name of humanity and decency" [the United States] should stop transferring Viet Cong prisoners to South Vietnamese units. . . .

"Probably more of these prisoners are executed than are permitted to survive," he told the Senate.

At the same time, Young said, the conscience of the world would find it revolting if North Viet Nam tried and executed American airmen held prisoner. . . . (p. 66.)

20 Jul. 66 *Cong. Record*—Senate, July 20, 1966, p. 15638.

MR. YOUNG of Ohio. Mr. President, the United States is signatory to the Geneva Convention requiring humane treatment of prisoners of war. . . . It has been our policy and practice throughout all our involvement in the miserable civil war raging in Vietnam to surrender and turn over to officers of the ARVN forces all Viet Cong prisoners of war we have taken. . . . It is well known that not only are these prisoners of war taken by Americans in combat mistreated following the time they are turned over to South Vietnamese authorities but also the facts are well known, that many of these prisoners of war are executed. Probably more of these prisoners of war are executed than are permitted to survive. How can we Americans evade responsibility for the mistreatment of these war prisoners? The Geneva Convention which had the all-out support of our Government, when provisions were written relative to humane treatment of prisoners of war and agreeing to those provisions, makes us responsible. (p. 66.)

7 Jul. 65 *New York Times:* Jack Langguth, Saigon, July 6.

During the Phugon battle last week, at least five Communist prisoners were shot because the capturing Government troops felt that they could not guard them properly. . . . One American helicopter crewman returned to his base in the central highlands last week without a fierce young prisoner entrusted to him. He told friends that he had become infuriated by the youth and had pushed him out of the helicopter at about 1,000 feet. (p. 71.)

Victor Charlie, by Kuno Knoebl, 1967.

. . . The interrogation of prisoners is usually rough in war. But in Viet-Nam it is often a matter of overwhelming cruelty. One method used to make a prisoner talk is to tie slipknotted cords around his throat and feet, so that if he moves, the noose around his throat slowly tightens. . . . Another method is to hang a captive by the feet over a rain barrel and slowly submerge him in it. He is not kept under long enough to drown at first; the process is repeated until the man talks or dies. . . . In the delta, South Vietnamese soldiers use the U.S. armored personnel carriers as instruments of torture. A Viet Cong is tied to the vehicle by a rope and slowly dragged through the rice paddies. A victim may survive being pulled through one or two of the water-covered fields, but he is dead by the third. (p. 77.)

. . . Most controversial of all is the practice of torturing prisoners, generally with electric shocks or smothering with wet towels. Murder and torture have been standard accessories to Viet Cong tactics for years. Prisoners are often killed outright or tortured to death. Troops on both sides are fond of beheading their enemies to get grisly trophies.

It is a war in which no quarter is given on either side.

America, deeply involved as it is in the Vietnamese conflict, has inevitably become involved in the "dirtier" sides of the war. U.S. advisors generally are somewhere around when prisoners are taken, and often witness ugly things. (p. 83.)

Destroying Huts and Villages

The Hague Convention of 1907, Article 23:

In addition to the prohibitions provided by special Conventions, it is especially forbidden—

(g) To destroy or seize the enemy's property, unless such destruction or seizure be imperatively demanded by the necessities of war. (p. 131.)

Article 53:

Any destruction by the Occupying Power of real or personal property belonging individually or collectively to private persons, or to the State, or to other public authorities, or to social or cooperative organizations, is prohibited, except where such destruction is rendered absolutely necessary by military operations. (p. 132.)

16 Sept. 65 *New York Times:* Charles Mohr, Camne, South Vietnam, Sept. 15.

. . . In early August a Marine battalion burned perhaps 500 houses in the embarrassing presence of a television crew.

. . . Around them is some evidence that the war is hard for the Vietnamese, too. Although Defense Department spokesmen had criticized the Columbia Broadcasting System for saying that 150 were burned in Camne, marines and Vietnamese officials insist that the correct figure was 500. (p. 139.)

22 Jan. 67 *Cleveland Plain Dealer:* John Bixler.

" . . . What I didn't like was when we burned the village down. The women and kids were crying and begging you not to burn them down. A lot of them stay inside and you have to drag them out.

"Ma, that's not good to see. I look back at what was once a village and the people crying, but as the sergeant told me, that's war. I guess he was right. It was a VC [Viet Cong] Village and we had to do it."

This is an excerpt from a letter from a U.S. fighting man in Vietnam, Sgt. Dennis Pena, to his parents, Mr. and Mrs. Benny Pena, 1601 Clark Avenue, S.W. (p. 140.)

Scorched Earth

20 Jan. 67 *New York Times* (Section 4).

Operation Cedar Falls, whose objective was to deny a sanctuary to the Viet Cong by laying it waste, was brought to a close last Thursday. It took place in the so-called Iron Triangle area of rubber plantations, scrub jungle, and paddy fields, totaling about 60 square miles, about 30 miles northwest of Saigon.

Whole villages were bulldozed and burned, and more than 6,000 persons—all but a handful, women, children and old men—were transferred to temporary camps under the threat of bombing. Miles of tunnels, laboriously dug by the guerrillas over a period of as much as 20 years, were explored and then blown up. They yielded truckloads of documents that are now being sifted by intelligence experts and expected to have a bearing on future American operations. Also seized were 3,709 tons of rice, more than enough to feed 10,000 men for a year, and 9,000 pounds of salt. Enemy dead were put at 720. (p. 147.)

27 Mar. 67 *Akron Beacon Journal:* Editorial and Letter to Editor.

Editorial: Americans at War.

More compelling, more graphic, than any editorial we have written about the war in Vietnam is the letter printed on this page today.

Here are the reactions of an Akron district boy—he could be that lad from across the street—who willingly donned the uniform to serve his country.

He is sickened and conscience-stricken at the murderous devastation he is ordered to commit.

Here is a father who is torn between loyalty to his country and frustrated anger that his son should be plunged into such a mess.

And the 16-year-old sister who just can't believe that her big brother could be killing defenseless people.

Is this the way the United States is "protecting" the rest of the world?

Read the letter—and weep.

Letter: We Burned Every Hut:

To the Editor:

Here are portions of a letter I have just received from my son, who is now stationed in Vietnam.

My son enlisted in the Army, asked to be sent to Vietnam and backed the government's strong policy toward the war in Vietnam—at least he did when he left this country last November. I believe what he has to say will be of interest to your readers:

"Dear Mom and Dad:

> "Today we went on a mission and I am not very proud of myself, my friends or my country. We burned every hut in sight!
>
> "It was a small rural network of villages and the people were incredibly poor. My unit burned and plundered their meager possessions. Let me try to explain the situation to you. . . ." (pp. 150–1.)

Use of Artillery

The Hague Convention of 1907, Article 25:

The attack or bombardment, by whatever means, of

towns, villages, dwellings, or buildings which are undefended is prohibited.

Article 26:

The officer in command of an attacking force must, before commencing a bombardment, except in cases of assault, do all in his power to warn the authorities. (p. 159.)

4 Jun. 64 Saigon, June 4.

. . . in the south, huge sectors of the nation have been declared "free zones," in which anything that moves is a legitimate target. Tens of thousands of tons of bombs, rockets, napalm and cannon fire are poured into these vast areas each week. If only by the laws of chance, bloodshed is believed to be heavy in these raids. (p. 179.)

Oct. 65 *New Republic:* Bernard B. Fall, "Vietnam Blitz."

. . . Indeed, as many informed observers in Saigon will concede, what changed the character of the Vietnam war was not the decision to bomb North Vietnam; not the decision to use American ground troops in South Vietnam; but the decision to wage unlimited aerial warfare inside the country at the price of literally pounding the place to bits. (p. 181.)

21 Nov. 65 *New York Times:* Editorial: "Bombing South Vietnam."

The increasing prospect of a long bitter struggle in South Vietnam—as revealed in the grim ground warfare of the Iadrang Valley—raises serious questions about an aspect of American strategy that has had too little public discussion. These questions arise out of the mounting ferocity of American air warfare in South Vietnam and the heavy damage it inflicts on South Vietnamese villages and the people who live in them. More sorties are now being flown by United States planes than in the Korean war, and the nature of guerrilla war makes it impossible to avoid killing innocent civilians as well as Vietcong. (p. 186–7.)

It is one thing to use air power in close support of ground forces when significant Vietcong units have been engaged.

It is quite another to wipe out villages remote from any specific combat area on the strength of reports—often ill-founded—that the Vietcong have been sheltered there. . . . In Vietnam itself more is involved than deaths, the carnage and the alienation of peasant loyalty. The bombs that destroy Vietnam's villages are smashing the social structure of the countryside. (p. 187.)

5 Mar. 67 *New York Times:* Tom Buckley, Saigon, South Vietnam, March 4.

. . . In fact, casualty figures are widely thought to have a great deal to do with the tactics that are most frequently employed by commanders here. It has been doctrine in the United States armed forces to use fire power instead of manpower in Vietnam. The wish to save American lives is based not only on humanitarian grounds, it is suggested, but also on domestic political considerations, since no one can quite be certain as to what the public response would be to several weeks of battle deaths in, say, the 500 range. (p. 204.)

Feb. 66 Air Force, "The Air War."

. . . The year-end tally, prepared last month at headquarters of the Second Air Division in Saigon, shows that during 1965 pilots flew almost 50,000 sorties. Of these, 10,570 were tactical strikes over North Vietnam and 37,940 over South Vietnam, in support of U.S. and Vietnamese army forces. On top of this, more than 1,000 B-52 sorties were launched from Guam.

Here are other vital statistics from the 1965 record:

USAF tactical pilots dropped 80,290 tons of bombs. The B-52 tonnage has not been disclosed.

VNAF pilots flew more than 23,700 tactical strikes, most of them in South Vietnam. They used 26,600 tons of bombs.

. . . In the South, all strikes were directed by the USAF Tactical Air Control Center (TACC) at Tan Son Nhut Air Base, near Saigon. TACC directed all pilots of USAF, the Navy, Marines and VNAF.

Air Force Forward Air Controllers (FAC), flying O-1 spotter planes, logged 10,330 missions in 1965. They also flew most of the 22,200 USAF visual reconnaissance flights.

USAF and VNAF strike pilots, hitting targets marked by the FAC, destroyed 80,330 Viet Cong buildings and damaged 44,390. They sank 1,756 sampans. It is estimated they killed more than 20,000 Viet Cong troops in the year. (p. 217.)

28 Jun. 65 *New York Times:* Jack Raymond, Bienhoa, South Vietnam, June 25.

. . . The fighter-bombers swoop into the target zone and bomb and strafe the base.

We also call it "skunk hunting," said Capt. John S. Lynch, an Air Force officer from Norfolk, Va.

. . . He added: "Day in and day out, whenever the weather permits—and sometimes even when weather is foul—we go skunk hunting. 'We are going on a skunk hunt,' the squadron commander will say, and everyone answers, 'Roger.' " (p. 230.)

Weapons

The Hague Convention of 1907, Article 23:

In addition to the prohibitions provided by special Conventions, it is especially forbidden—

(a) To employ poisoned weapons.

(b) To kill treacherously individuals belonging to the hostile nation or army.

(e) To employ arms, projectiles, or material calculated to cause unnecessary suffering. (p. 29.)

25 Mar. 65 Saigon, Viet Nam (The M-16).

. . . Other weapons used by American and Vietnamese forces also have become controversial. One of these weapons is the .223-caliber Armalite rifle, introduced in combat for the first time in Viet Nam.

The rifle has a muzzle velocity so high that its metal-jacketed bullet virtually explodes when it hits a human being, causing a huge jagged wound. The effect is similar to the Dum-Dum expanding bullet outlawed by the Geneva Convention. (p. 271.)

2 Jan. 67 *Journal of the American Medical Association:* "Wounding Power of Missiles Used in the Republic of Vietnam."

. . . Another factor to be considered in the wounding power is attributed to what is termed the "tumbling effect" of the M-16 bullet. The marked difference in the wound entrance and exit size that is usually seen was demonstrated in one patient with an 0.5-cm entrance wound on the anterior area of the thigh and a 4 x 8-cm exit wound on the anterior of the leg. There is often a characteristic minute lead splatter from the soft core after the copper jacket fragments, and this is seen frequently on roentgenograms. Bone involvement, usually in the form of severe comminuted fractures, was seen in the majority of these wounds; trauma to nerves, arteries and veins was common. Included are injuries to the internal jugular vein, the superficial femoral artery, the external ilian vein, and the median and ulnar nerves. (p. 272.)

Hanson Baldwin, military editor of the *New York Times,* in a dispatch carried on May 1, 1966, reported that Vietnam is a proving ground for new weapons, never before used in combat:

. . . Many anti-personnel weapons of various types have also been tried with air dispensers—from bomblets and dart to a modern variety of cannister. (p. 276.)

3:

Policeman of the World

When the United Nations Charter was adopted in June 1945, nations of diverse ideologies believed that they had devised a means for establishing a rule of law in the international arena. When the United States and the Soviet Union agreed to be bound by the terms of the Charter, neither believed that the other reserved to itself the right to use armed force in situations in which such use was forbidden to it.

The United Nations Charter specifically demanded that "all members shall refrain in their international relations from threat or use of force against the territorial integrity or political independence of another state."

In spite of our commitment to the Charter, which, when adopted by the Senate, became the law of our land, President Truman bypassed it when he adopted the "containment policy," later known as the Truman Doctrine. In effect, this policy made the United States the policeman of the world.

The President promulgated his policy of containment on March 12, 1947, at a joint session of Congress. The essence of this "containment of communism" doctrine was that the United States would underwrite with its economic resources and its military manpower the defense of all states everywhere in the world that were threatened by "aggressive movements that seek to impose on them totalitarian regimes."

The provocation for the announcement of the Truman Doctrine was the conclusive representation in February 1947 by the British Foreign Office to the United States State Department that Great Britain could not continue its financial assistance to Greece. As a consequence, the Foreign Office believed, the Greek Government would fall when British military forces were withdrawn at the end of 1947.

President Truman enunciated his doctrine as follows:

> At the present moment in world history nearly every nation must choose between alternative ways of life, the choice is now often not a free one. . . . I believe that it must be the policy of the United States to support free peoples who are resisting attempted subjugation by armed minorities or by outside pressures. . . . The world is not static, and the status quo is not sacred. . . . But we cannot allow changes in the status quo by such methods as coercion or by subterfuge or political infiltration.[1]

At the time this policy was formulated, nationalism was asserting itself all over the globe. The rule of imperial domination was giving way. The British Empire was becoming reconciled to the emergence of independent states—India, Pakistan, Burma, Ceylon, Nepal, Afghanistan, and Palestine. Revolutionary movements were challenging the domination of the French in Indochina and of the Dutch in Indonesia. Vacuums were being created where formerly colonial enclaves had existed. In Greece and Turkey, whose governments the United States was planning to assist when

President Truman spoke, revolutionary forces were seeking to dislodge reactionary rulers.

A. Intervention in Korea

At the end of World War II the Korean Peninsula was divided along the Thirty-eighth Parallel. American observers in South Korea reported in June of 1950 that North Korean armed forces were attacking.

On June 27, President Truman ordered "United States Air and Sea forces to give the Korean government troops cover and support." On the same day, the United States called upon the Security Council of the United Nations to invoke sanctions against North Korea, and recommended "such assistance to the Republic of Korea as may be necessary to repel the armed attack, to restore international peace and security in the area." [2]

The United States experience during the thirty-nine months of warfare on that peninsula was not very reassuring. In 1954, in his official announcement to the Senate of the signing of the armistice agreement which brought the Korean war to an end, Senator William Knowland declared:

> While we should appreciate the token contribution of 35,000 men from 17 of the 60 members of the United Nations, neither we nor they should misrepresent to the American people or to the free world, that this example represents the effective collective security action. It does not.[3]

Historians of the Korean war have indicated that four-fifths of the cost of the police action in Korea was borne by the United States.

Lieutenant General James M. Gavin, in an appearance before the Senate Foreign Relations Committee in February 1966, said, "I don't think we did well in Korea. I don't think our readiness was anywhere near what it should have been." [4]

Furthermore, the extent to which the Korean episode was, in essence, a United States operation is borne out by the fact that in Korea the United States Army alone totaled 1,600,000,[5] whereas, according to Senator Knowland, the other seventeen nations combined contributed not more than 35,000.

The truce in Korea has often been referred to as the Eisenhower peace. When President Eisenhower was campaigning for the presidency in 1952, he committed himself to bringing about peace in Korea. That "peace" he achieved in June of 1953, when the Korean armistice was signed. It is therefore understandable that he refused to become involved militarily in the Vietnam conflict when the French suffered their disastrous defeat at Dienbienphu in May of 1954.

Our involvement in Vietnam, where we are mired down with an armed force of approximately a half million, can be understood only if the Vietnam war is recognized as a chapter in the history of an American policy that has continued ever since President Truman enunciated his containment of communism doctrine in 1947.

The following incidents, most of which preceded our military involvement in Vietnam in February 1965, illuminate the tragic consequences to which we are heir unless the foreign policy enunciated in the Truman Doctrine is abandoned.

B. The 1954 Guatemala Incident

In 1954, relations were deteriorating between the United States and the Guatemalan administration under President Jacobo Arbenz Gusman. The United Fruit Company, whose holdings in Guatemala were substantial, was affected by the land-reform laws which were adopted. The disputes with the United Fruit Company became the focus of anti-American feelings in that country.

In May of 1954, information reached the American Government that the Swedish S. S. *Alfhen,* carrying a cargo of several tons of arms from Europe, was on its way to Guatemala. The British Ambassador in Washington was advised by Secretary of State John Foster Dulles that the United States Navy had been ordered to establish what amounted to a blockade of the Guatemalan coast. Orders were issued that all suspicious vessels were to be searched for arms, with permission of the government concerned, *if* there was time to obtain it.

Anthony Eden, in his memoirs, recounts this episode, indicating that the British Government "could not possibly acquiesce in forcible action against a British ship without its permission." Mr. Dulles was unable to give Britain the assurance it sought. In fact Dulles observed that "in the cold war conditions of today, the rules applicable in the past no longer seemed to him to meet the situation and required to be revised or flexibly applied." [6]

Professor Henry Steele Commager, when he appeared before the United States Senate Committee on Foreign Relations on February 20, 1967, stated:

> You will bear with me if I remind you of what you doubtless know, that in 1954 we established, on our own, a

> blockade of Guatemala, as we attempted to avoid what we thought was a Communist takeover in that country. We have recently been informed, by documents just now published, that at the time of this blockade American planes bombed and severely damaged a British ship approaching Guatemala.

In the opinion of textbook writers on international law, the U.S. blockade constituted an act of war. And when the blockade was coupled with an incident resulting in severe damage to a ship approaching Guatemala, it constituted an act of aggression. Manifestly this is an exercise of the police power which is the consequence of compliance with the Truman containment policy.

C. The 1958 Lebanon Incident

In 1958, because of the sudden collapse of the government of Iraq, a group of dissident forces within Lebanon began to challenge President Camille Chamoun's regime. Armed uprising in Lebanon appeared imminent. President Chamoun appealed for help. We had no treaty with Lebanon. There appeared to be no subversion from without, as was envisioned by the Truman Doctrine, yet the United States found it possible to dispatch an armada of American ships and planes to Beirut and ultimately to land 2,500 Marines to assist President Chamoun.

This invasion was clearly a violation of international law. If a civil war was threatened in Lebanon, American forces had no justification for assisting either side in the internal strife. During our own Civil War the British did not dare go to the assistance of the Confederates, even though they sympathized with them.

Professor Quincy Wright, one of America's most distinguished professors of international law, in a contribution to the *American Journal of International Law* entitled "United States Intervention in Lebanon," stated:

> . . . interventions in the form of military reprisals to rectify wrongs when peaceful methods fail, while permissible by customary international law before World War I, have been forbidden by conventional obligations in the League Covenant and the Kellogg-Briand Pact, and particularly by the obligation of members of the United Nations "to settle their international disputes by peaceful means." [7]

The Lebanon incident not only represented a form of aggression but certainly exemplified the police action contemplated by the Truman Doctrine.

D. The Cuban Incident of 1962

During the latter part of 1962 there came to President Kennedy's attention the fact that dangerous atomic missiles were being stored in Cuba. His administration, after serious deliberations, concluded that the presence of those Russian-owned and Russian-supervised atomic missiles was a menace to our security. Without a declaration of war and almost on forty-eight hours' notice, a blockade of Cuba was ordered. All Russian vessels, as well as all other vessels, were ordered to avoid Cuban waters, and thus the encirclement of the island of Cuba by the American Navy became complete. This act on the part of the United States Government was in direct violation of the Charter of the Organization of American States.

Article 15 of that Charter reads:

> No state or group of states has the right to intervene, directly or indirectly, for any reason whatever in the internal or external affairs of any other. The foregoing principle prohibits not only armed forces but also any other form of interference or attempted threat against the personality of the state or against its political, economic or cultural elements.

Article 16 reads:

> No state may use or encourage the use of coercive measures of an economic or political character in order to force the sovereign will of another state and obtain from it advantages of any kind.

Whether textbook writers consider a quarantine of a whole country an act of aggression is not really the point. Any act which, by means of force, interferes with the right of another state to maintain its sovereignty is an act of aggression.

The Cuban incident illustrates a situation in which the United States engaged in a police action even in the face of its own commitment under a regional treaty not to use coercive measures "in order to obtain advantages of any kind." (See Appendix C.)

E. The Dominican Republic Incident of April 1965

General Rafael Trujillo Molina had ruled the Dominican Republic with an iron hand from 1930 until his assassination in 1961. In 1962, Juan Bosch, a liberal reformer, was elected President in the first free election held in that country in thirty-eight years. In September 1963, Bosch was overthrown and his regime was replaced by an army-backed civilian triumvirate led by Donald Reid Cabral.

On April 24, 1965, a revolt was launched by followers of Juan Bosch and others. This uprising, which was popular in nature, sought to restore Bosch to power. But on April 28, the United States landed 24,000 troops in the Dominican Republic.

There was no claim of aggression, direct or indirect, by another power. There was no threat of invasion to subvert the government of the Dominican Republic. While there may have been disputes among various factions within the Republic, there was no appeal for assistance by any faction. The original explanation for our landing the Marines was that their sole purpose was to protect the lives and property of Americans. It was only after they were present in the Republic that President Johnson found it possible to issue a statement, on May 2, 1965, saying that "Communist conspirators" had become dominant in the rebellion and that the "American nation cannot, must not and will not permit the establishment of another Communist government in this hemisphere."

The Communist-oriented government of Fidel Castro, which came into power January 1, 1959, did not appear to threaten the security of the United States from the time of its establishment up to and even including the missile incident of November 1962. The Castro government was still in power under the same Communist-oriented form of government in April 1965. The landing of the Marines in the Dominican Republic was a clear violation of Articles 15 and 16 of the Charter of the Organization of American States. It constituted an intervention in the internal affairs of another sovereign state, an act of aggression proscribed by the O.A.S. Charter.

The Dominican incident is a clear demonstration of the conduct of the United States as policeman of the universe, in an area close to home.

By way of explanation, a brief economic-political interpretation of some of these incidents may be useful.

The blockade of Guatemala was in no small measure inspired by the land-reform laws enacted by President Arbenz. In the first months of 1954, more than 100,000 families had benefited from the agrarian reform, which affected only idle lands. Only eight percent of the land owned by the United Fruit Company had been cultivated by that company. Soon after the invasion of Guatemala, Washington officially conceded that Castillo Armas, who led the invading force from Honduras, had been trained at Fort Leavenworth, Kansas, and that North American volunteers had piloted the B-47 bombers. It was, according to some commentators, a C.I.A. job. What is perhaps not coincidental is that General Walter Bedell Smith, one of the heads of the C.I.A., joined the board of directors of United Fruit, one of whose chairs had already been occupied by the current No. 1 man of the C.I.A., Mr. Allen Dulles.[8]

The intervention in Lebanon was also not unrelated to American economic interest in the stability of the Bagdad Pact countries. When the King of Iraq and his adviser, Nuri-es-Saed, were assassinated, the threat to Lebanon became imminent. American and British oil holdings were threatened. President Chaumoun of Lebanon appealed for protection, and received it. This invasion of Lebanon has much kinship with the C.I.A. coup in Iran, when Mossadegh was pushed out. As soon as Mossadegh was ousted, his successor promptly gave twenty-five-year leases on 40 percent of Iran's oil to three U.S. oil firms. One of these was Gulf

Oil. Mr. Kermit Roosevelt, on the C.I.A. payroll and not a stranger to the Mossadegh ploy, became, in 1960, a vice-president of Gulf Oil.

The Dominican Republic invasion by more than 20,000 Marines sent "to save American lives and property" is also not free of substantial economic interest. At stake in the Dominican Republic was the "Caribbean Sugar Bowl." Ellsworth Bunker, Jr., at present United States Ambassador to South Vietnam, was profoundly involved in the Dominican invasion. Mr. Bunker's interest is not unrelated to the fact that he is a board member and stockholder of the National Sugar Refining Company, a firm his father founded. Ambassador Averell Harriman's brother Roland is also a member of the board of the National Sugar Refining Company. The former United States Ambassador to the Dominican Republic, Joseph Farland, is a board member of the South Puerto Rican Sugar Company, which owns 175,000 acres of rich land in the Dominican Republic and is the largest employer on the island at one dollar a day per man.[9]

The United States is similarly committed on a world-wide basis, as evidenced by the scope of military spending. Data made available by the National Security Research Project of the Institute for Policy Studies shows that in 1968 two-thirds of all federal tax receipts were spent for military and war-related costs. Military spending exceeded the profits of all American businesses and totaled more than federal, state, and local governments spent on health, education, old-age retirement assistance, housing, and agriculture. The United States operated 450 overseas bases containing 1,751,000 military personnel at a maintenance cost of about $4.8 billion a year. The Defense Department purchases almost 15 percent of the finished products of all

U.S. industries and over 18 percent of all industrial durable goods. Ties between the military establishment and industry—as well as ties with politicians—are close. The 100 biggest defense contractors now employ 2,072 former officers with the rank of colonel, Navy captain, or higher. This is almost three times the number on their payrolls ten years ago.[10]

Professor Seymour Melman, an authority on military spending, in a memorandum to the Senate Armed Services Committee, stated that the current (1970) Pentagon budget is based on: "1. war in the NATO area; 2. a war in the China area; 3. a lesser military action in Latin America." This constitutes a requirement that U.S. armed forces be capable of fighting wars in each of these areas at the same time—conducting one nuclear war and two conventional wars at once. This combination of military operations does not refer to the defense of the United States.

While the above Pentagon perspective broadly suggests the roles of both gendarme of the universe and magistrate of the universe, it also envisages a blanketing of "Pax Americana" over the globe.

The extent to which the United States is committed to maintain "peace" on a world-wide basis was revealed by Secretary of State Dean Rusk when he appeared before the Senate Foreign Relations Committee on February 18, 1966:

> *Senator Aiken:* And are we bound to fight communism wherever it exists?
> *Secretary Rusk:* No, sir, no, sir, we are not. We are not talking about fighting communism for the purpose of destroying communism as such, as a social or political organization. But what we are talking about, I believe, Senator, is that where communist countries undertake to

> commit aggression against those to whom the U.S. has undertaken a clear commitment in an alliance, that there we have a duty to assist our allies to meet that aggression.[11]

At the same hearing, Secretary of State Rusk listed the forty countries in the world to which the United States had made such a commitment. Among these are:

> The North Atlantic Treaty, which includes some fifteen nations as follows: United States, Canada, Iceland, Norway, United Kingdom, Netherlands, Denmark, Belgium, Luxembourg, Portugal, France, Italy, Greece, Turkey, Federal Republic of Germany.
>
> The Rio Treaty, which includes twenty-one nations: United States, Mexico, Cuba, Haiti, Dominican Republic, Honduras, Guatemala, El Salvador, Nicaragua, Costa Rica, Panama, Colombia, Venezuela, Ecuador, Peru, Brazil, Bolivia, Paraguay, Chile, Argentina, Uruguay.
>
> The Anzus Treaty, which includes three nations: United States, New Zealand, Australia.
>
> The Philippine Treaty, a bilateral treaty with the Philippines.
>
> The Republic of Korea Treaty, a bilateral treaty with the Republic of Korea.
>
> The Southeast Asia (SEATO) Treaty, which includes eight nations: United States, United Kingdom, France, New Zealand, Australia, Philippines, Thailand, Pakistan.
>
> The Republic of China Treaty, a bilateral treaty with the Republic of China (Formosa).
>
> The Japanese Treaty, a bilateral treaty with Japan whereby Japan requests, and the United States agrees, to "maintain certain of its armed forces in and about Japan . . . so as to deter armed attack upon Japan." [12]

Since at this moment in history the United States maintains a military force of more than 250,000 in Germany, 55,000 in Korea, 50,000 in Thailand, 540,000 in Vietnam, as well as one and a half million military personnel at 450 overseas bases, the basic affirmation of Pax Americana has been made. A careful examination of our annual national budget will also disclose that a substantial number of the forty countries with whom we have these binding alliances are also beneficiaries of U.S. nonmilitary aid programs.

On January 1, 1968, *U.S. News & World Report* published a pictograph of the globe in which it depicted U.S. bases flying the American flag. The accompanying story indicated that over a million and a half of our American forces were engaged abroad. The figure is broken down as follows:

In the Southeast Asia battle zone	550,000
Elsewhere in the Far East	217,000
In the Caribbean	23,000
In Europe and the Mediterranean	352,000
Elsewhere abroad, in naval fleets or en route	400,000

In the Pacific and the South China Sea, the United States has twelve major bases; in the Caribbean, four bases; and in the Atlantic and European theaters, twelve bases.

Secretary of State Rusk, in his appearances before the Senate Foreign Relations Committee in January and February of 1966, disavowed the implications that Pax Americana is being imposed. In view of such commitments of servicemen and military bases, it is hard to imagine what the Secretary would have considered an implication of a Pax Americana policy. Perhaps we need not leave it entirely to historians to determine whether, by 1969, the United States had actually acted as a policeman of the world and whether Pax Americana had already been imposed.

4:

The Background of Our Involvement in Vietnam

French Indochina was a colonial possession of France for almost eighty years. Vietnam was one of several entities that were encompassed by that colony. The thirty million Vietnamese were not strangers to invaders, but they also retained a tradition of fighting outsiders, whether they were Mongols, Chinese, French, or Japanese.

During the Japanese occupation, which ended September 2, 1945, an exiled underground fighter named Ho Chi Minh became the rallying agent for various underground factions. On the day of the Japanese collapse he released the Declaration of Independence of the Democratic Republic of Vietnam. Modeled after the United States Declaration of Independence of 1776, it began with the sentence, "All Men Are Created Equal."

The French, after V-J Day, in their zeal to retrieve the colony and re-establish their domination of Indochina, even resorted to the use of Japanese soldiers. This brazen act elicited the following remarks from General Douglas A. MacArthur:

> If there is anything that makes my blood boil, it is to see our Allies in Indochina and Java deploying Japanese troops to reconquer these little people we promised to liberate. It is the most ignoble kind of betrayal.[1]

It must be remembered that tin and rubber are two of the valuable natural resources of that part of the world, and that the French were eager to maintain their monopoly. U.S. economic interests were not blind to the natural wealth of Indochina either, and as U.S. financial aid began to flow into that part of the world, U.S. aims began to reveal themselves. The *New York Times* of February 12, 1950, discloses some of them:

> Indochina is a prize worth a large gamble. Ever since World War II, Indochina has yielded an annual interest of 300 million dollars. In the North are exportable tin, tungsten, zinc, manganese, coal, lumber, and rice, and in the South are rice, rubber, tea, pepper, cattle, and hides. . . . From the military standpoint Indochina is equally important, forming an 800-mile long bridge between Communist China and British Malaya and with a common frontier with both Burma and Thailand. Its two main harbors, Hai Phong and Saigon, are excellent bases.

On March 13, 1952, Robert S. Lovett, Secretary of Defense, advised Congress of the importance of Indochina for the United States by stating:

> The strategical, geographical position of the area, as well as the vitally important raw materials, such as tin and rubber, which it supplies, makes it important for us to maintain an effective support of the French Government.

And in July of 1953, the Inquiry Committee of the United States Aid Commission reported the following to the House of Representatives:

> Now let us assume that we lost Indochina. If that happened, the tin and tungsten that we do greatly value from that area would cease coming. . . . So when the United States votes 400 million dollars to help that war, we are not voting a give-away program. We are voting for the cheapest way that we can to prevent the occurrence of something that would be of a most terrible significance to the United States of America, our security, our power and ability to get certain things we need from the riches of the Indochinese territory and from South East Asia.

France recognized the Republic of Vietnam as a "Free State" within the French Union. An election to determine Vietnam's status as a "Free State" was promised to Ho Chi Minh by the French, but that promise was never kept.

During the period of the French reoccupation a struggle began in Vietnam. The French set up Bao Dai as their head of government, and in 1950 the Soviet Union and the newly created Communist government in China both recognized Ho Chi Minh as the head of the Democratic Republic of Vietnam.

U.S. aid to the French in Indochina continued. Between 1950 and 1954 it totaled approximately $2 billion.[2] This aid continued during the U.S. involvement in Korea. In 1953 the French military situation began to deteriorate. When President Eisenhower took office in January 1953, the importance that his new administration attached to preserving Indochina as a French possession was shown in many ways. For example, his Secretary of State, John Foster Dulles, in a speech on July 17, 1953, declared, "What we have done in Indochina will save us from having to spend much more money to protect our vital interests in the Pacific," and on September 2, 1953, at a meeting of the National Committee of the American Legion in St. Louis, Missouri, he said:

> In Indochina a desperate struggle is in its eighth year. The outcome affects our vital interests in the western Pacific and we are already contributing largely in material and money to the combined efforts of the French, and of Viet Nam, Laos, and Cambodia.

By January 27, 1954, the United States Embassy in Saigon reported that:

> . . . from 1950 to December 1953, the U.S. has supplied France with more than 400,000 tons of war material, including 1,400 tanks, 340 planes, 350 warships, 15,000 radio sets, 150,000 weapons, 240,000 rounds of small arms ammunition and 15,000,000 other cartridges.

The French military position became desperate. On March 20, 1954, the French Chief of Staff, General Paul Ely, advised President Eisenhower that only massive American intervention could prevent a defeat of the French at Dienbienphu. If such intervention were not forthcoming, then France would be obliged to negotiate a settlement with the Vietminh (Ho Chi Minh's forces).

The sharp arguments that ensued in Washington during the siege of Dienbienphu are of special interest today, because their outcome temporarily spared the American people the anguish of another Korea.

The debate over intervention in support of the French in Vietnam saw Admiral Arthur Radford, Chairman of the

5:

United States Intervention in Vietnam Is Illegal

In March 1965, only a month after our bombardment of North Vietnam had commenced, the United States Government apparently deemed it necessary to justify its unilateral action in Vietnam, and the State Department issued a memorandum entitled "Legal Basis of U.S. Action Against North Vietnam."

A careful reading of the document convinced a group of American lawyers that our military involvement in Vietnam was in violation of international law, including the United Nations Charter.

In consultation with leading authorities in the field of international and constitutional law, a Memorandum of Law, "American Policy Vis-à-Vis Vietnam," was prepared by the Lawyers Committee on American Policy Towards Vietnam. This Memorandum, which reviewed the conclusions of the State Department treatise, was endorsed by professors of law from the University of Virginia, Columbia, Yale, Princeton, Cornell, and other law schools, as well as by attorneys in private practice.

The regrettable but inescapable conclusion of the Lawyers Committee was that the action of the United States in Vietnam contravened the essential provisions of the United Nations Charter, to which the United States is bound by treaty; violated the Geneva Accords of 1954, which the United States pledged to observe; was not sanctioned by the treaty creating the South East Asia Treaty Organization; and violated the United States Constitution's provision that only Congress can declare war.

The Committee's Memorandum of Law, which was published in the Congressional Record of September 23, 1965, was distributed to every active member of the bar and to the professors of law at the universities. On January 25, 1966, it was forwarded to President Johnson and Secretary of State Rusk.

On March 4, 1966, a little more than a year after the United States became militarily involved in Vietnam, the Legal Adviser to the Department of State released a fifty-two-page Memorandum of Law entitled "The Legality of the United States Participation in the Defense of Vietnam." [1] This State Department Memorandum in essence constituted a reply to the Memorandum of Law that had been prepared and distributed by the Lawyers Committee on American Policy Towards Vietnam.

To prepare a thoroughly documented answer to this second State Department memorandum, the Lawyers Committee on American Policy Towards Vietnam invited scholars who concerned themselves with international law and government to serve as a consultative council to their committee and to undertake the preparation of an analysis of the Legal Adviser's Memorandum of March 4, 1966. (The members of the Consultative Council are listed in Appendix C.)

It should be noted that among the university faculties

represented in the Consultative Council are those of Princeton, Harvard, and the University of Virginia. The Consultative Council represents more than a fair share of the most eminent, established, and well-recognized authorities on international law in the American academic community. As a group, they are objective scholars without partisan commitment to any particular segment of the American political structure.

The Consultative Council set forth its findings in a memorandum entitled "The Military Involvement of the United States in Vietnam: A Legal Analysis." *

The issue of the legality of United States intervention in Vietnam has precipitated many debates since the publication of the various memorandums cited above. It seems desirable now to summarize the debates in terms of traditional international law, of the United Nations Charter, and of the accords and treaties in which the United States is a participant. The observations that follow are based upon articles by the author (see Appendix A), and, more particularly, upon the legal analysis set forth in the treatise entitled "Vietnam and International Law," which was prepared by the Consultative Council of the Lawyers Committee on American Policy Towards Vietnam.

A. U.S. Intervention in Vietnam Violates the Geneva Accords of 1954

The Geneva Conference, which began April 26, 1954, and ended July 21, 1954, was called essentially to resolve

---

* This memorandum was published in book form under the title *Vietnam and International Law* (Flanders: O'Hare Books, 1967).

problems in Southeast Asia that had demanded solution ever since the defeat of Japan.

Because all five of the Great Powers were concerned with an agreement on Indochina, the conference was uniquely structured. Participants were the United Kingdom, France, the United States of America, the Union of Soviet Socialist Republics, and the People's Republic of China—and, in addition, the Democratic Republic of Vietnam, Laos, and Cambodia.

The Korean war had not yet been resolved.

On May 7, 1954, France suffered a decisive defeat at Dienbienphu and the conference began to concern itself with the conditions under which France would be permitted to withdraw from Vietnam in order not to make its exodus humiliating.

On July 20, the agreement on the cessation of hostilities in Vietnam was consummated. This agreement was made possible only after M. Mendès-France took office as Premier on June 18, with a commitment to the French electorate that he would terminate France's involvement in Indochina. The agreement was signed by the French Commanding Officer in behalf of the Commander-in-Chief of the French Union Forces in Indochina, and by the Vice-Minister of National Defense of the Democratic Republic of Vietnam in behalf of the Commander-in-Chief of the Army of Vietnam.

This agreement on the cessation of hostilities provided that the division of Vietnam at the Seventeenth Parallel was only "a provisional military demarcation," on either side of which the opposing forces could be "regrouped"—"the forces of the People's Army of Vietnam to the north of the line and the forces of the French Union to the south." (Chapter I, Article 1 of that agreement.) [2]

The Geneva agreement makes plain the fact that the division of the Seventeenth Parallel was to be temporary, to enable the French forces to depart in an orderly fashion, and that appropriate steps were to be taken for the holding of a general election of a government for a unified nation. Pending the election, "civil administration in each regrouping zone [was to] be in the hands of the party whose forces are to be regrouped there" (Article 14(a)).

The agreement also provided that "the signatories of the present agreement and their successors in their functions shall be responsible for ensuring the observations and enforcement of the terms and provisions thereof."

During the Geneva Conference, Bao Dai, the designee of France during the period between 1945 and 1954, at the suggestion of the new colonialists (the United States), persuaded Ngo Dinh Diem to become premier of his government. Diem was strongly nationalist, anti-French, and anti-Communist. It appears he was not altogether unknown to the U.S. administration which had been so generous in its aid to France before the fall of Dienbienphu.

The provisions of the agreement about the responsibility of the signatories to enforce its terms become especially important when we assess Ngo Dinh Diem's role during the years between 1954 and his assassination in 1962.

The day after the agreement on the cessation of hostilities was consummated, all the participants took part in what came to be known as the Final Declaration of the Geneva Conference on the Problems of Restoring Peace in Indochina. The Final Declaration is contained in thirteen distinct paragraphs.[3]

In Paragraph 4 of the declaration, the participants took "note of the clauses in the agreement on the cessation of hostilities in Vietnam prohibiting the introduction in Vietnam of foreign troops and military personnel, as well as of all kinds of arms and ammunition."

In Paragraph 6, the participants recognized that "the essential purpose of the agreement relating to Vietnam is to settle military questions with a view to ending hostilities and that the military demarcation line is provisional and should not in any way be interpreted as constituting a political or territorial boundary."

In Paragraph 7 it is provided that "In order to ensure that sufficient progress in the restoration of peace has been made and that all the necessary conditions obtain for free expressions of the national will, a general election shall be held in July 1956, under the supervision of an International Commission composed of representatives of all member states of the International Supervisory Commission, referred to in the agreement on the cessation of hostilities. Consultations will be held on this subject between the competent representative authorities of the two zones from July 20, 1955, onwards."

After the Final Declaration had been fully set forth, the representatives of the participating nations were called upon by the chairman (Mr. Eden). Undersecretary of State Walter Bedell Smith, representing the United States, addressed the chairman and his fellow delegates to the effect that the government of the United States was resolved to devote its forces to the strengthening of peace in accordance with the principles and purposes of the United Nations. Preliminarily, Mr. Smith took note of the accords which had been concluded on July 20 and 21; he then declared that the United States would "refrain from threats or the use of force to disturb them, in accordance with Article 2 (4) of the Charter of the United Nations dealing with the obligation of members to refrain in their international relations from the threat or use of force. . . ."

Referring to the elections in Vietnam, the United States declaration states: "In the case of nations now divided against their will, we shall continue to seek to achieve unity through elections supervised by the United Nations, to ensure that they are fairly conducted."

Nowhere in its own declaration did the United States recognize the political partition of Vietnam. Both agreements and the unilateral declaration by Undersecretary Smith referred to Vietnam as a whole.

The United States further pledged that "it will not join in any arrangements which will hinder" the unification of Vietnam, and concluded with the hope that the agreement would "permit Cambodia, Laos, and Vietnam to play their part in full independence and sovereignty in the peaceful community of nations, and will enable the peoples of the area to determine their own future."

No election was ever held pursuant to the Geneva Accords, although both the International Commission (composed of India, Poland, and Canada) and the United Nations announced readiness to supervise such elections.

Ngo Dinh Diem knew that if an election were held it would be a popularity contest between himself and Ho Chi Minh, and he knew that Ho would quite likely win. Ho was far better known as the leader in the fight against France; he had an aura of success about him.

The esteem in which Ho Chi Minh was held by the people of Vietnam in 1955, immediately after the consummation of the Geneva Accords, was acknowledged by former President Dwight D. Eisenhower, who in his memoirs gave his reason for Diem's refusal to hold elections.

> I have never talked or corresponded with a person knowledgeable in Indochina affairs who did not agree that, had an election been held at the time of the fighting, possibly 80 percent of the population would have voted for the Communist Ho Chi Minh as their leader rather than Chief-of-State Bao Dai.[4]

The Geneva Accords embodied two central principles: 1) the recognition of the independence and freedom of Vietnam from foreign control; and 2) the unification of the two zones in elections in 1956.

Diem defended his refusal to agree to an election by saying that neither his government nor the United States had agreed at Geneva to the elections and therefore neither was bound by that agreement.

This statement runs counter to the terms of the July 20, 1954, Geneva agreement, both because Bao Dai and his chosen Premier, Diem, acceded to the terms of the agreement signed by France on cessation of hostilities, and because Undersecretary Smith had in fact agreed to elections being held under the supervision of the International Supervisory Commission.

As the time for election arrangements approached, however, the Diem regime, which was then in control of the territory south of the Seventeenth Parallel, announced (on July 16, 1954) that it would not only defy the provisions calling for national elections, but would refuse to even engage in negotiations for modalities.

In spite of the fact that nowhere in the Geneva Accords nor in Undersecretary Smith's declaration is there any statement of what conditions must prevail before elections can take place, on August 31, 1955, Secretary of State John Foster Dulles declared that the conditions required to proceed to general elections in Vietnam were not yet mature, and approved the position of the Saigon administration, which had refused consultation with the government of the Democratic Republic of Vietnam on this subject.[5]

President Eisenhower, in a letter to Diem dated October 23, 1954, expressed readiness to give aid to him:

> The purpose of this offer is to assist the Government of Vietnam in developing and maintaining a strong, viable state, capable of resisting attempted subversion or aggression through military means. The Government of the United States expects that this aid will be met by performance on the part of the Government of Vietnam in undertaking needed reforms. It hopes that such aid, combined with your own continuing efforts, will contribute effectively toward an independent Vietnam, endowed with a strong Government. . . .

It must be noted that in this letter President Eisenhower directed his aid to Diem in the hope that it would "assist the Government of Vietnam in developing and maintaining a strong, viable state." In October of 1954, Eisenhower clearly did not give aid to Diem as a head of government. Nevertheless, a year later, on October 26, 1955, Ngo Dinh Diem declared South Vietnam a Republic. This declaration that the zone below the Seventeenth Parallel was an independent government was clearly a further violation of the Geneva Accords.

It is fair to assume that Mr. Diem would not have refused to hold elections if he had not believed his refusal would be supported by the United States. Discussions to work out election arrangements were scheduled by the Geneva agreement to begin July 20, 1955, between the "competent representative authorities of the two zones." Diem flatly refused to cooperate, stating on July 16, 1955, "We have not signed the Geneva Agreements. We are not bound in any way by these Agreements, signed against the will of the Vietnamese people." The United States clearly supported Diem in this stand.[6]

As successor to the French forces in Victnam, Diem knew that he was bound by the terms of the Geneva agreement on cessation of hostilities to hold an election. He knew also that the International Commission, set up under that agreement, would insure conditions for a free election. So, of course, did the White House and the State Department. It may well be that Diem's refusal to hold an election, and U.S. support of his position, triggered the civil war in Vietnam which resulted in United States involvement there.

The United States military intervention in Vietnam violates the second essential of the Geneva Accords, the prohibition against foreign troops and military bases. Since Article 4 prohibits the introduction into Vietnam of foreign troops and military personnel, and Article 5 prohibits any military base under the control of a foreign power, it would appear that the presence of more than half a million American troops and the installation in Vietnam of masses of military bases under the control of the United States violate these agreements.

As late as September 18, 1961, the International Control Commission still insisted upon the obligation to hold elections for reunification. In a special report on June 1, 1962, the I.C.C. declared that the United States' "increased military aid" to South Vietnam and its "factual military alliance" with South Vietnam violated the Geneva Accords.

However, aid to South Vietnam continued at an ever-increasing pace throughout the years that Diem was in control of what he was pleased to call the Republic of Vietnam. The legal and moral corruption of Diem's regime increased, and his usefulness as a conciliator in Vietnam came to an abrupt end. What motivated his assassination in 1963, and who specifically was responsible for it, remains a mystery to this day. The fact remains however, that his effectiveness as a head of government had terminated, and his assassination on November 1, 1963, was almost expected. Although Diem, as successor to the French Union Forces of Indochina (one of the parties to the July 21, 1954, Accord), was obliged to honor the terms of the Geneva agreement, he consistently honored them in the breach rather than the observance.

B. U.S. Intervention Violates the SEATO Treaty

The SEATO Treaty was signed at Manila on September 8, 1954, only forty-nine days after the Geneva Accords had been consummated.

In July 1954, during a recess of the Geneva Conference, Prime Minister Winston Churchill and Foreign Secretary Anthony Eden conferred in Washington with President Eisenhower and Secretary Dulles. Although, according to Mr. Eden's memoirs (p. 161), most of the Washington conclave was devoted to discussing Korea and Vietnam, on July 17th a study group was set up in Washington to draft a document which would consider "possible measures of collective defense for South East Asia and the South West Pacific."

It was suggested in Washington that the five Colombo powers—India, Pakistan, Ceylon, Burma, and Indonesia—be asked to participate in the consideration of the measures that would be submitted to a contemplated Manila Conference. Pakistan was the only member of the Colombo powers that agreed to attend.

The SEATO Treaty was, therefore, signed by the United States, Great Britain, France, Australia, New Zealand, the Philippines, Pakistan, and Thailand.

President Johnson, in a speech at Johns Hopkins University on April 7, 1965, declared that we were in Vietnam because "we have made a national pledge to help South Vietnam defend its independence. And, I intend to keep that promise."

The commitment to defend Vietnam, according to White House and State Department hindsight, is based upon an undertaking in the South East Asia Defense Treaty. This Treaty was signed on September 8, 1954. It should be noted that in July 1954, when the American representative at Geneva promised U.S. agreement to "refrain from the threat or use of force to disturb" the Geneva Accords, there was no *South Vietnam* in existence, only a *Vietnam*. The State Department's Memorandum of Law of March 1965, "The Legal Basis for United States Action Against North Vietnam," did not mention the SEATO Treaty, nor was there any mention of it in Johnson's speech at Johns Hopkins on April 7.

Significantly, too, President Johnson, in a press conference statement on July 28, 1965, explaining "why we are in Vietnam," made no mention of SEATO. This can hardly be squared with the belated claim that the Treaty imposed an obligation upon the President to intervene in Vietnam.

The claim of obligations under SEATO is therefore discredited by its belatedness and, more specifically, because it assumes a commitment to a sovereign or international entity that was not a party to the agreement.

When Secretary of State Dean Rusk stated "It is a fundamental SEATO obligation that has from the outset guided our actions in South Vietnam,"[7] his observation came somewhat belatedly.

Futhermore, a week after the United States Air Force attacked North Vietnam, Ambassador Henry Cabot Lodge was interviewed as follows:

> Q.: Recently, questions have been raised in this country about the legal aspects of what we are doing in Vietnam; what is our justification under international law?
> Lodge: To me the legal aspect of it is the least significant.
>
> Q.: Is this an international action in Vietnam?
> Lodge: It is a fact that the action we are taking in Vietnam is not under the aegis of any international organization. *It is not under the aegis of the United Nations or the South East Asia Treaty Organization—SEATO.* It is a relationship between us . . . the United States and the government of Vietnam. We were invited by the government. [Emphasis added.][8]

It was not until March 4, 1966, more than a year after the United States took its unilateral action against North Vietnam, that the State Department claimed to rely upon the SEATO Treaty. That was the day the State Department issued "The Legality of the United States Participation in the Defense of Vietnam."[9]

In early 1955, during the Senate debates on ratification of the SEATO Treaty, Senator Walter F. George, Chairman of the Senate Committee on Foreign Relations, explained the extent to which the United States was being committed under the SEATO Treaty:

> The treaty does not call for automatic action; it calls for consultation with other signatories. If any course of action shall be agreed . . . or decided upon, then that action

> must have the approval of Congress, because the constitutional process of each signatory government is provided for . . . it is clear that the threat to territorial integrity and political independence also encompasses acts of subversion . . . but even in that event the United States would not be bound to put it down. I cannot emphasize too strongly that we have no obligation . . . to take positive measures of any kind. All we are obligated to do is consult together about it.[10]

Senator H. Alexander Smith, one of the senators who was a member of the American delegation to the Manila Conference at which SEATO was negotiated and who was one of the signers of the Treaty, emphasized that nothing in the Treaty calls for the use of American ground forces:

> Some of the participants came to Manila with the intention of establishing . . . a compulsory arrangement for our military participation in case of any attack. Such an organization might have required the commitment of American ground forces to the Asian mainland. We carefully avoided any possible implication regarding an arrangement of that kind.
>
> We have no purpose of following any such policy as that of having our forces involved in a ground war. . . .
>
> For ourselves the arrangement means that we will have avoided the *impracticable overcommitment* which would have been involved if we attempted to place American ground forces around the perimeter of the area of potential Chinese ingress into southeast Asia. Nothing in this treaty calls for the use of American ground forces in that fashion. [Emphasis added.][11]
>
> The Treaty (SEATO) does not call for automatic action: it calls for consultation with other signatories. . . . I cannot emphasize too strongly that we have no obligation to take positive measures of any kind. All we are obliged to do is to consult together about it.[12]

And finally, during the hearings on SEATO, Secretary Dulles engaged in some significant exchanges about the full meaning of SEATO:

> *Senator Green:* Then we are obliged to help put down a revolutionary movement.
> *Secretary Dulles:* No, if there is a revolutionary movement in Vietnam or in Thailand, we would consult together as to what to do about it, because if that were a subversion that was in fact propagated by communism, it would be a very grave threat to us. But we would have no undertaking to put it down. All we have is an undertaking to consult as to what to do about it. . . .
> *Senator Ferguson:* In other words, the words "armed attack" in paragraph 1 of Article IV are the ordinary armed attack rather than a subterfuge of penetration or subversion?
> *Dulles:* Yes, sir.[13]

What is also telling is that during these hearings, Secretary Dulles explained to the Senate, ". . . Article 4, page 2, contemplates that if that situation [of subversion] arises or threatens, that we should consult together immediately in order to agree on measures which should be taken. This is an obligation for consultation; it is not an obligation for action." [14]

The SEATO Treaty does not enlarge the legal basis for the use of force contained in the United Nations Charter. The State Department Memorandum of March 4, 1966, misleadingly asserts that the Treaty's Article 4, subsection 1, creates an "obligation to meet the common danger in the event of an armed aggression."

The term "armed aggression" is not contained in the Treaty. Repeating the language of the United Nations Charter, Article 4 speaks of "aggression by means of armed attack." Since "armed attack" had not occurred, SEATO could not authorize defensive action. If "armed attack" had occurred, SEATO would have been redundant, as the use of force is then permissible under Article 51 of the United Nations Charter.

Furthermore, in the event of "armed attack," the United States would have had, at most, the legal *right,* but certainly not the *obligation,* to assist South Vietnam. None of the other SEATO parties regarded military intervention in Vietnam as legally required by SEATO. On the contrary, two leading members of SEATO, Pakistan and France, have publicly denounced the United States role in the Vietnam war.

The extent to which the members of SEATO consider themselves obligated to participate in the defense of Vietnam was further revealed at Senate Foreign Relations Committee hearings which were conducted in January and February of 1966, and in which Secretary of State Dean Rusk, Lieutenant General James M. Gavin, General Maxwell D. Taylor, and former Ambassador George F. Kennan participated. Senator Mundt expressed disappointment at the results of U.S. efforts to bring in support from countries that should have some concern about what is happening in Vietnam.

At that point, Secretary Rusk submitted a long statement of the assistance given to the United States in Vietnam. A summary of this assistance appears in the very useful volume *The Truth About Vietnam:*

> Applying this principle ["reciprocity"] to Vietnam, we find that the obligation under SEATO becomes a self-imposed one, apparently without any reciprocal obligation by our Treaty partners. We have 300,000 men involved in this conflict, counting those serving in the Seventh Fleet.

> According to the Department of Defense, our 7 SEATO Treaty partners had a legal total of some 1600 men in Vietnam as of January 15, 1966: Australia had 1400; New Zealand had 150; Thailand had 17; the United Kingdom had 12; the Philippines had 70; France and Pakistan had none and will never have any because they do not support our policy.[15]

The question of the legality of U.S. intervention in Vietnam has been a matter of deep concern to diplomats and students of international law. On April 21, 1967, addressing the House of Commons, Mr. Philip Noel-Baker, one of England's most distinguished diplomats, a member of successive British cabinets and winner of the Nobel Peace Prize, observed:

> President Johnson and Mr. Rusk sometimes say they were compelled by their SEATO obligations to intervene. But if they were to look at the Treaty they would see that, by Article I, Article IV, and Article VI, the SEATO Pact specifically and categorically forbids what the United States has done. Every day that the war continues the whole concept of world order based on law is progressively undermined.

Article 1 of the SEATO Treaty provides that:

> The parties undertake, as set forth in the United Nations Charter, to settle any international disputes in which they may be involved, by peaceful means . . . and to refrain in their international relations from the threat or use of force in any manner inconsistent with the purposes of the United Nations.

Article 4, Section 2, is explicit in stating that if Southeast Asia were threatened "in any way other than by armed attack, the [SEATO] parties shall consult immediately in order to agree on the common defense."

It should be pointed out that Article 53 of the United Nations Charter provides that "no enforcement action shall be taken under regional arrangements or by regional agencies, without the authority of the Security Council." And Article 103 provides, "In the event of a conflict between the members of the United Nations under the present Charter and their obligations under any other international agreement, their obligations under the present Charter shall prevail."

It seems clear that even if the United States had obtained the required consent of the other SEATO powers, authorization from the United Nations Security Council would still have been required to establish the legality of the United States action.

Therefore, the United States, far from being "obligated," is not permitted by SEATO or by the United Nations Charter to engage in its military undertaking in Vietnam.

On July 1, 1970, President Nixon in his conversation with the representatives of the major news networks stated quite emphatically, in response to inquiries as to whether the United States would recommit manpower to Cambodia, that, in effect, no United States forces would return to Cambodia. However, he indicated that if an ally were to be attacked to whom we owed contractual commitments, there is a good likelihood that we would fulfill our contractual obligations. Clearly, President Nixon had our SEATO commitments to Thailand in mind.

On July 5th, less than a week after American forces committed to Cambodia had been withdrawn, Secretary of State William P. Rogers participated at Saigon in the annual meeting of the SEATO "allies." It must be particularly noted that two of the Asian members (the Philippines and

Pakistan) and France were not represented. The only SEATO members present were Thailand, South Korea, Australia, New Zealand, and the United States. A *New York Times* reporter, in commenting on the progress of the talks, observed that "the United States officials said that Thailand, who they had hoped would send ground troops to Cambodia, had so far reached no 'political decision' to do so." [16]

Thus it appears that the one Asian member of SEATO present at the meeting on July 5th, namely Thailand, was unwilling as of that day to commit any forces to Cambodia. Clearly implied is Thailand's unwillingness to become involved and to possibly be used as an excuse for further United States aggression in Southeast Asia.

This posture of Thailand vis-à-vis Cambodia reflects ominously on President Nixon's statement to the major news networks representatives that he would consider himself bound to come to the aid of a country to whom we had made contractual commitments.

Although President Nixon did not state that the commitment made to Thailand was that made under the SEATO agreement, there is no commitment that he could have been referring to, other than that of SEATO. Although he was cautiously indirect, what President Nixon was really saying to the American people was that reescalation in Southeast Asia is not only a possibility but a probability—and that the justification would be our SEATO commitment to Thailand.

C. The Unilateral Intervention of the United States Violates the United Nations Charter

The right of collective "self-defense" under Article 51 of the Charter arises only if an armed attack has occurred. The phrase "armed attack" has an established meaning in the Charter and in international law. "Self-defense" is not justified by every aggressive or hostile act, but only in the case of an "armed attack," when the necessity of action becomes "instant, overwhelming and leaving no room for deliberation."

Article 51 provides, "Nothing in the present Charter shall impair the inherent right of individual or collective self-defense if an armed attack occurs against a member of the United Nations, until the Security Council has taken measures to maintain international peace and security."

The provisions of this Article constitute a serious restriction on the traditional right of self-defense. Professor Philip C. Jessup, at present a member of the International Court of Justice, in his book *Modern Law of Nations,* explains:

> Article 51 of the Charter suggests a further limitation on the right of self-defense. It must be exercised only "if an armed attack occurs," . . . This restriction in Article 51 very definitely narrows the freedom of action which states had under traditional law. A case could be made out for self-defense under the traditional law where an injury was threatened but no attack had as yet taken place. Under the Charter, alarming military preparations by a neighboring state would justify a resort to the Security Council, but would not justify a resort to anticipatory force by the state which believed itself threatened.[17]

Professor Hans Kelson, in his book entitled *The Law of the United Nations,* makes the following comment on the full meaning of collective self-defense:

> It is important to note that Article 51 does not use the term "aggression" but the much narrower concept of "armed attack," which means that . . . a common act of aggression which has not the character of an armed attack involving the use of force does not justify resort to force.[18]

Thus if one is to assume that South Vietnam has an "inherent" right to self-defense, it does not mean that the United States has the right to decide to participate unilaterally in that defense.

Professor Jessup also argues, under Article 51 of the Charter, against interference by outside powers in situations comparable to that of Vietnam. He observes, "It would be disastrous to agree that every state may decide itself which of the two contestants is in the right and may govern its conduct according to its decision." [19]

Article 51 also requires that measures taken by members in the exercise of their right of self-defense shall be *immediately* reported to the Security Council. According to the definition both in the Charter and under traditional international law, there has been no armed attack justifying United States intervention. Nor has the Security Council been called upon to determine whether there has been any threat to the peace, breach of the peace, or aggression.

Published statements and official declarations of the State Department justifying intervention in Vietnam are predicated on the premise that North Vietnam has been guilty of aggression against the South. This claim, it would seem, is challenged by the historical record.

On January 6, 1966, Mike Mansfield, the majority leader

of the Senate, submitted a report to the Senate Foreign Relations Committee entitled "The Vietnam Conflict: The Substance and the Shadow." [20] This report reveals that before 1965, infiltration from the North "was confined primarily to political cadres and military leadership." On the other hand, it notes that by 1962 U.S. military advisers and service forces in South Vietnam totaled approximately 10,000 men. The Mansfield report also makes plain that significant armed personnel were introduced from the North only after the United States had intervened, when "total collapse of the Saigon Government's authority appeared imminent," in the early months of 1965:

> United States combat troops in strength arrived at that point in response to the appeal of the Saigon authorities. The Vietcong counter-response was to increase their military activity with forces strengthened by intensified local recruitment and infiltration of regular North Vietnamese troops.[21]

In an address at Yeshiva University, in New York, on June 16, 1966, Senator Mansfield declared, "When the sharp increase in the military effort began in early 1965, it was estimated that about 400 North Vietnamese soldiers were among the enemy forces in South Vietnam which totaled 140,000 at that time." [22]

It has been claimed that United States intervention in Vietnam is sanctioned under Article 51 on the grounds that 1) South Vietnam is an independent state; 2) South Vietnam has been the victim of an armed attack from North Vietnam; and 3) the United States, with the consent of South Vietnam, is engaged in "collective self-defense" of that country, as claimed by the United States in a communication to the United Nations Security Council in March of 1965.[23]

To sustain this claim, *all three* elements must be satisfied. The claim is untenable on several grounds. First, South Vietnam was not recognized as an independent state at the 1954 Geneva Conference. Even if it had become a de facto state in the course of events since 1954, infiltration from North Vietnam could not be deemed to constitute an "armed attack" within the special language of Article 51.

Second, since the Geneva Accords recognized all of Vietnam as a single state, the conflict of either the Vietcong or Ho Chi Minh against the Saigon Government is "civil strife," and foreign intervention is forbidden because civil strife is a domestic question—a position insisted upon by the United States in its Civil War of 1861.

With respect to the claim of "collective self-defense" in Article 51, the question arises whether the United States can validly be a genuine member of a regional system covering Southeast Asia. Articles 51 and 53 of the Charter, dealing with regional systems, were intended primarily to integrate the inter-American system with the United Nations organization. The idea that the United States—a country separated by oceans and thousands of miles from Southeast Asia, and having no historical or ethnic connection with the people of Southeast Asia—could validly be considered a member of a regional system implanted in Southeast Asia is utterly alien to the regional systems envisaged in the Charter.

Remembering the Colombo powers' refusal to participate in the Manila Conference which produced SEATO, we are not surprised that the majority of the eight SEATO members are representatives of Western culture, and that the only non-Western members are Pakistan, Thailand, and the Philippines. Pakistan has openly indicated its disapproval of the intervention, and Thailand and the Philippines are by now recognized as client subordinates of the United States.

Article 103 of the United Nations Charter plainly accords supremacy to that Charter, making all members of the United Nations primarily obligated to comply with its provisions. The commitment to SEATO by the United States, Great Britain, and France—all permanent members of the Security Council—appears to be in open disregard of the stern language of the United Nations Charter.

It would seem that a fair study of the United Nations Charter affirms the observations of Professor Louis Henkin of Columbia University, when he spoke of "the law of the Charter":

> So far as it purports to prescribe for the conduct of nations, it consists, basically, of one principle: *Except in self-defense against armed attack,* Members must refrain from the threat or use of force against other states. . . . the rule of the Charter against unilateral force in international relations is the essence of any meaningful concept of law between nations and the foundation on which rests all other attempts to regulate international behavior. . . .[24] [Emphasis added.]

The inescapable conclusion, therefore, is that the action of the United States in Vietnam contravenes the essential provisions of the United Nations Charter. Nowhere in the literature on the Vietnam war is it seriously urged that the Pleiku attack, which precipitated the bombing of North Vietnam on February 7, 1965, constituted in any manner an *armed attack* which warranted the devastating, unrestrained attack upon the Vietnamese people.

The Pleiku area is located in the central part of South Vietnam. The U.S. garrison at Camp Holloway, which was located in the Pleiku area, consisted of special forces. The attack at Pleiku was carried out at night by South Vietnamese guerrillas against American barracks, killing eight Americans and wounding 126. How this typical night raid on an encampment in the center of South Vietnam could be construed as an *armed attack* of "overwhelming" proportions that left "no moment for deliberation" is difficult to comprehend, unless it constituted an "awaited" act excusing massive retaliation.

There has been no armed attack justifying United States intervention as defined in the Charter and declared in traditional international law. Nor has the Security Council been called upon to determine the existence of any threat to the peace, breach of the peace, or act of aggression.

D. United States Intervention Violates the Constitution

It is the genius of the constitutional system that ours is a government of checks and balances. The fundamental doctrine of the separation of powers is one of the "great structural principles of the American constitutional system."[25]

The Supreme Court, in *United States* v. *Brown,* stated:

> The power to make necessary laws is in Congress; the power to execute, in the President. Both powers imply many subordinate powers. Each includes all authority essential to its due exercise. But neither can the President, in war more than in peace, intrude upon the proper authority of Congress, nor Congress upon the proper authority of the President. (*Ex parte Milligan,* 1866) 381, U.S. 437.

In Article 1, Section 8, clause 11 of the Constitution, the power to declare war is confided exclusively to the Congress. There is no mention of the President in connection with the power to "declare" war. Under the Constitution, Congress alone must make this decision. The clause affecting the power to declare war does not read, "On the recommendation of the President," or "The President with the advice and consent of Congress may declare war."

Former Assistant Secretary of State James G. Rogers has observed: "The omission is significant. There was to be no war unless Congress took the initiative." [26]

That the President lacks the constitutional power to make war was explicit in President Woodrow Wilson's statement when he addressed Congress on April 2, 1917. He told the joint session:

> I have called the Congress into extraordinary session because there are serious, very serious, choices of policy to be made, and made immediately, which it was neither right nor constitutionally permissible that I should assume the responsibility of making.

Nowhere in the debates on the adoption of the Federal Constitution is there to be found any language which in any way suggests that the President can wage a war or "commit" our nation to the waging of war.

The Constitutional Convention was not only determined to deny war-making powers to the President, but was also unwilling to entrust it to the Senate alone. To ensure the fullest consideration, the framers of the Constitution provided that the House of Representatives, larger and more representative than the Senate, should also be brought in to decide this vital question.

President Johnson, however, took the position that the Southeast Asia Resolution (Tonkin Resolution) of August 10, 1964, is the clear and unequivocal congressional sanction of the President's deployment of United States forces in South Vietnam.*

It seems more likely that the action of Congress under the conditions that prevailed when the Tonkin Resolution was submitted constitutes, at most, an ultimatum, not a declaration of war. Senator Fulbright, in "The Fatal Arrogance of Power," a lead article in the *New York Times* Magazine of May 15, 1966, wrote:

> The joint resolution was a blank check signed by the Congress in an atmosphere of urgency that seemed at the time to preclude debate. . . .
>
> I myself, as chairman of the Foreign Relations Committee, served as floor manager of the Southeast Asia resolution and did all I could to bring about its prompt and overwhelming adoption. I did so because I was confident that President Johnson would use our endorsement with wisdom and restraint. I was also influenced by partisanship: an election campaign was in progress and I had no wish to make any difficulties for the President in his race against a Republican candidate whose election I thought would be a disaster for the country. My role in the adoption of the resolution of Aug. 7, 1964, is a source of neither pleasure nor pride to me today.

There have been other instances when a President has sent forces abroad without a declaration by Congress. These have ranged from minor engagements between pirates and American ships on the high seas to the dispatch of our armed forces to Latin American countries and our involve-

---

* The misinterpretation by Johnson with regard to the mandate granted to him under the Tonkin Resolution is fully exposed by the action taken by the Senate on June 24, 1970, repealing that resolution. This act, in and by itself, establishes the illegality of our presence in Vietnam.

ment in Korea. But except for the Korean war, none of these instances involved nearly so massive and dangerous a military undertaking as the war in Vietnam. And in the Korean war, the United States did obtain the aegis of the United Nations.

In the opinion of some, the Tonkin Resolution constitutes a congressional declaration of war. It is permissible to recall that on May 4, 1954, at a time when the fall of Dienbienphu was imminent, Senator Lyndon B. Johnson criticized President Eisenhower in these terms:

> We will insist upon clear explanations of the policies in which we are asked to cooperate. We will insist that we and the American people be treated as adults—that we have the facts without sugar coating.
>
> *The function of Congress is not simply to appropriate money and leave the problem of national security at that.* [Emphasis added.]

An attempt by Congress to transfer its power and responsibility to make war to the President would be unconstitutional and unauthorized and would destroy the political system envisaged by the framers of the Constitution.

The Tonkin Bay Resolution, however, is not a declaration of war. It "approves and supports the determination of the President as Commander-in-Chief to take all necessary measures to repel any *armed attack* against the forces of the United States and to prevent further aggression." [Emphasis added.] But it also provides that all such steps shall be "consonant with the Constitution of the United States and the Charter of the United Nations and in accordance with its obligations under the Southeast Asia Collective Defense Treaty."

It is clear that the congressmen who voted for the Tonkin

Bay Joint Resolution were not voting a declaration of war in Vietnam. The resolution does not mention North Vietnam, nor China; indeed, it does not even mention Vietnam. It was "passed in the fever of indignation that followed reported attacks by North Vietnamese torpedo boats against United States fleet units in Tonkin Bay." [27]

There is no evidence that Congress thought or understood that it was declaring war. It took no contemporaneous action which would have implemented a declaration of war. Congress manifestly cannot delegate to the President its exclusive power to declare war; and even under the specific terms of the Tonkin Resolution, it did not intend to do so. Under our system, constitutional powers must be exercised in a constitutional manner by constitutionally established institutions.

On March 10, 1954, President Eisenhower was questioned at a news conference about the danger of becoming involved in the Indochina war. He replied: "I will say this, there is going to be no involvement of America in war unless it is the result of the constitutional process that is placed upon Congress to declare it. Now let's have that clear. And that is the answer." (See Appendix B for a fuller treatment of this point.) [28]

6:

Who Are the Aggressors?

What constitutes aggression has perplexed writers ever since books on international law were first written. The United Nations has been trying to define it since its inception and, after many years of inaction, on December 18, 1967, the United Nations finally established the "Special Committee on Defining the Question of Aggression." [Resolution 2330 (XXII).]

When this "Special Committee" met in Geneva in June 1968, four draft proposals on aggression were introduced. It met again in New York during the 1969 meeting of the General Assembly, on March 25, 1969. At this meeting the United States, United Kingdom, Canada, Australia, Italy, and Japan submitted a draft proposal defining aggression which, in part, reads as follows:

> I. Under the Charter of the United Nations, "aggression" is a term to be applied by the Security Council when appropriate in the exercise of its primary responsibility for the maintenance of international peace and security under Article 24 and its functions under Article 39.
>
> II. The term "aggression" is applicable, without prejudice to a finding of threat to the peace or breach of the peace, to the use of force in international relations, overt

> or covert, direct or indirect, by a State against the territorial integrity or political independence of any other State, or in any manner inconsistent with the purposes of the United Nations.[1]

In order to arrive at an understanding of who, in fact, were aggressors in the Vietnam war, now in its "escalated" phase for more than five terrible years, it is important to examine certain conditions that existed before Lyndon Johnson's assumption of the presidency of the United States.

In 1945, when World War II ended in Asia, the United States and Great Britain undertook to help France retrieve its colonial losses. These colonies included not only Vietnam but Cambodia and Laos. On September 2, 1945, Ho Chi Minh, who had led the Vietnam resistance movement during the Japanese occupation, tendered the Declaration of Independence of the *Democratic Republic of Vietnam.* This new sovereignty claimed the right to govern the section of the French Indochina possession known as Vietnam. The French colonial forces called that same section of Indochina the State of Vietnam, and designated Bao Dai as the head if the *State of Vietnam.*

The civil war that ensued raged from 1945 to 1954. During the last two years of that war, United States taxpayers paid over 80 percent of the French cost of that war, expending some $2 billion in aid.

After the French surrendered at Dienbienphu in May 1954, the Vietnamese forces under Ho Chi Minh were literally in complete control.

Under the Geneva Accords of July 1954, an election was to have taken place to determine specifically whether the Democratic Republic of Vietnam under Ho Chi Minh would govern Vietnam (both North and South) or whether some other Vietnam government would prevail. That election, as we have already seen, was never held. On October 26, 1955, Ngo Dinh Diem declared that South Vietnam would thereafter be known as the Republic of Vietnam.

Thus, it would appear that in the winter of 1964 a civil war had been in progress for about ten years in the section of Vietnam below the Seventeenth Parallel, with the National Liberation Front and the Saigon regimes as the contending forces.

Throughout the Eisenhower and Kennedy regimes, almost unrestrained financial and military aid was extended to Saigon. President Eisenhower had promised that the United States would aid Vietnam in every way possible, except militarily, and in September 1963, exactly two months before President Diem was assassinated, President Kennedy said:

> In the final analysis, it is their war. They are the ones who have to win it or lose it. We can help them, we can give them equipment, we can send our men out as advisors, but they have to win it—the Vietnam people—against the Communists. . . . All we can do is help, and we are making it very clear.[2]

The position of the Eisenhower administration vis-à-vis U.S. involvement in Vietnam has been summarized as follows:

(1) No American arms in Asia, no land war in Asia;
(2) No commitments to aid colonialism or to suppress nationalism in Asia;
(3) In any event, no unilateral military intervention; and resort to force only under some international sanction, in particular, the U.N.;
(4) Any multilateral commitment to force should be

made in a specific area, for a specific limited purpose, in order to keep the conflict localized;

(5) Specifically in South Vietnam, the supplying of aid–money, supplies, arms—but not U.S. armies.[3]

The nonmilitary aid given during the Eisenhower administration to Bao Dai and to the Ngo Dinh Diem regime before the French capitulation at Dienbienphu was substantial. However, the extent and the form of aid given by the United States after Dienbienphu is not without significance. For instance, during the year 1958 two U.S. construction companies, Johnson Drake & Piper and Capital Engineering Corporation, constructed a whole network of strategic roads linking Saigon with the city of Ban Me Thuot, as well as other strategic military highways.

In addition, U.S. military missions of high-ranking officers visited Saigon. Among these officers were General I. D. White, Commander-in-Chief of U.S. land forces in the Pacific, and General George Decker, Commander-in-Chief of the U.S. forces in Korea. On December 31, 1959, Admiral Arthur Radford, former Chairman of the Joint Chiefs of Staff, also visited Saigon.

Such aid is quite inexplicable if it is recognized that the struggle after the departure of the French was, in effect, a civil war. Therefore, to the extent that both President Eisenhower and President Kennedy felt free to give financial and military aid, including advisers, to the Saigon regime, it must be realized that the aid given to the National Liberation Front by the Vietnamese north of the Demilitarized Zone was equally legitimate and permissible, and that all the aid which came to the National Liberation forces from China and the Soviet Union, and which was transported by the Vietnamese down the Ho Chi Minh Trail, was equally legitimate aid.

It must also be recognized that, if the Hanoi regime sent military advisers south of the D.M.Z. to aid the National Liberation Front in the use of military equipment given to them as aid, the presence of these Hanoi advisers was no less legitimate than that of American military advisers who accompanied the U.S. aid given to the Saigon government in South Vietnam.

On the question of whether or not the North Vietnamese were guilty of aggression, it is permissible to refer again to the report submitted to the Foreign Relations Committee by Senator Mike Mansfield, entitled "The Vietnam Conflict: The Substance and the Shadow," in which he stated that before 1965 the infiltration from the North "was confined primarily to political cadres and military leadership." And in his address at Yeshiva University on June 16, 1966, Mansfield declared that in early 1965, when the "sharp increase" in the military effort began, it was estimated that only about "400 North Vietnam soldiers" were among the forces in the South, "which totaled 140,000 at that time."

If, therefore, we rely on Senator Mansfield's statements, we must conclude that "before 1965" there was no movement south from the North of such appreciable military force as to warrant the bombardment that was begun on February 7, 1965.

President Johnson's decision to "stop aggression from the North" by an open act of war in February 1965 should be judged in the light of his declarations not only after he became President, but also when he was Vice-President.

President Johnson's order to bomb Vietnam has been called a "mistake," a "blunder," and a "miscalculation." Whether or not the misjudgment was arrant is a matter that historians will evaluate. We should turn to the record. As far back as May 1961, Vice-President Johnson was requested by President Kennedy to investigate conditions in Southeast Asia. Upon his return he prepared a memorandum for the President in which he observed:

> The fundamental decision required of thc United States —and time is of the greatest importance—is whether we are to attempt to meet the challenge of Communist expansion now in Southeast Asia by a major effort in support of the forces of freedom in the area or throw in the towel. This decision must be made in a full realization of the very heavy and continuing costs involved in terms of money, of effort, and of U.S. prestige. *It must be made with the knowledge that at some point we may be faced with the further decision of whether we commit major U.S. forces to the area or cut our losses and withdraw* should our efforts fail. *We must remain master of this decision.* [Emphasis added.] [4]

Thus it appears that during the early days of his Vice-Presidency, Johnson investigated the possibility that "we may be faced with the further decision of whether we commit major U.S. forces to the area." Even then his thoughts seem to have been directed toward the inevitability of our becoming involved in a shooting war—in the nature of aggression.

In December 1963, less than a month after he took his oath of office, in a New Year's message to General Duong Van Minh, who had succeeded Diem as head of the Saigon Government, President Johnson announced:

> . . . The United States will continue to furnish you and your people with the fullest measure of support in this bitter fight. We shall maintain in Vietnam American personnel and material as needed to assist you in achicving victory.
>
> Our aims are, I know, identical with yours: to enable

> your government to protect its people from the acts of terror perpetrated by Communist insurgents from the north. As the forces of your government become increasingly capable of dealing with this aggression, American military personnel in South Vietnam can be progressively withdrawn.
>
> The United States Government shares the view of your government that "neutralization" of South Vietnam is unacceptable. As long as the Communist regime in North Vietnam persists in its aggressive policy, neutralization of South Vietnam would only be another name for a Communist takeover. Peace will return to your country just as soon as the authorities in Hanoi cease and desist from their terrorist aggression.
>
> . . . I know from my own experience in Vietnam how warmly the Vietnamese people respond to a direct human approach and how they have hungered for this in their leaders. So again I pledge the energetic support of my country to your government and your people.[5]

These statements sharply define Johnson's belief that American involvement required an open-end military commitment. That this view was openly shared by members of his Cabinet is clear from a speech by Secretary of Defense Robert L. McNamara, made on March 26, 1964:

> The U.S. role in South Vietnam then is, *first,* to answer the call of the South Vietnamese, a member nation of our free-world family, to help them save their country for themselves; *second,* to help prevent the strategic danger which would exist if Communism absorbed Southeast Asia's people and resources; and, *third,* to prove in the Vietnamese test case that the free world can cope with Communist "wars of liberation" as we have coped successfully with Communist aggression at other levels.[6]

The administration's thinking, spearheaded by the President, was obviously more concerned with the Communist threat of wars of liberation than with proposed acts of aggression from the North.

The following facts reveal the administration's purpose and perspective: General Minh, who succeeded Premier Diem in 1963, was soon replaced by General Khanh in January 1964. According to the Senate report referred to above, when Secretary of Defense McNamara testified before the Senate Committee on February 18, 1964, he still insisted that the "bulk" of U.S. troops would be pulled out by the end of 1965.

In July 1964, when General Westmoreland succeeded to the command of the United States Military Advisory Commission in South Vietnam, our advisory body had grown to 23,000, but the South Vietnamese whom they came to advise appeared to be melting away.

During the year 1964, before the U.S. attack on North Vietnam, ten different governments quickly succeeded one another in Saigon. South Vietnam was almost completely disorganized. According to one report, during the winter of 1964–65 the South Vietnam army dwindled to slightly over 200,000 men. They had lost by desertion or to the Communists almost a third of their strength.

The full meaning of this critical posture vis-à-vis the Saigon regime and the United States Military Advisory Corps pointed not to a withdrawal of U.S. forces but, rather, to the prevention of "the strategic danger which would exist if Communism absorbed Southeast Asia's people and resources," the second concern set out by Secretary McNamara in his speech of March 26, 1964.

Chapter Two of this book quotes some of the stern "determinations" to which President Johnson committed himself with regard to sending our young people into a land war in Asia. These hypocritical utterances by a President cannot be misunderstood or easily forgotten. That the members of his Cabinet and his administration were preparing at the time for an inevitable war or an act of aggression cannot be denied.

The request for and swift passage of the Gulf of Tonkin Resolution of August 7, 1964, provides dramatic proof. The accuracy of the reports of the presumed Communist torpedo boat attacks on the SS *Maddox* and the SS *Turner Joy* has since been challenged by senators who participated in almost unanimously adopting the Gulf of Tonkin Resolution.

Senator Albert Gore made this observation about the unseemly haste with which the Senate was called upon to act:

> I feel that I was misled; that this was an entirely unprovoked attack, that our ships were entirely on routine patrol. The fact stands from today that they were intelligence ships; that they were under instructions to agitate the North Vietnam radar, that they were plying close to the shore, within 4 miles of the islands under orders in the daytime, retiring at night; that they were covered with immediate air cover which, in itself—that they were covered with military aircraft which you said on television the other day, which would be provocative off of North Korea. Why it would not be provocation of North Vietnam I do not know.[7]

The Congressional Record of August 6, 1964 (pages 18423–35), reveals that one senator, a member of the Foreign Relations Committee, felt, even at the time, that he was released from his obligation of secrecy (July 31, 1964), for he said that "United States presence in the [Tonkin Bay] area was thus bound to be regarded by the North Vietnamese as 'provocation.' "

The Johnson administration's chicanery in rushing the Tonkin Gulf Resolution through the Senate is also pointed out in statements made by two highly regarded Washington newspapermen. One of them, in his weekly publication, quoted a Saigon newspaper to the effect that there was a sharp step-up of the South Vietnam commando raids on northern territory as early as *July 10, 1964*—more than three weeks before the torpedo boat attack which provoked the Tonkin Resolution.[8]

The other Washington reporter, now an associate editor of the *New York Times,* in an article about President Johnson's political behavior, commented:

> Usually the timing is precisely [Johnson's] own, as when he presented his Vietnam Resolution [Tonkin Bay Resolution] to Congress on the day after the Gulf of Tonkin crisis. *He had been carrying it around in his pocket for weeks waiting for the moment.* [Emphasis added.] [9]

The Senate report of May 9, 1967, issued by the Senate Republican Policy Committee, states that "by March 1964, newspaper accounts described Vietnamese reluctance to take U.S. military advice and described the difficulties we were facing in getting the Vietnamese troops to fight." [10]

Although the South Vietnamese themselves seemed unwilling to do battle, by July 1964 the Advisory Corps which the United States had dispatched to Saigon to insure the proper use of our military aid was not the only U.S. military contingent in Vietnam. This Senate report states that in July 1964 the war was costing the United States $1.5 million a day. In the meantime, announced troop strength in Vietnam had climbed to 18,000. Thus U.S. "troop strength," combined with the "Advisory Body" of 23,000 men, was making a substantial contribution to the military strength on the Saigon side of the South Vietnam Civil War.

In evaluating U.S. intervention in Vietnam as an act of aggression, it is also important to note that while Johnson was campaigning for the presidency in the summer of 1964, Premier Khanh's regime in Saigon was cracking wide open; and that two years later, on February 20, 1966, the *New York Times* made this astonishing statement: "In the summer of 1964 Premier Khanh was promised a bombing offensive against the North, presumably on Presidential authority."

Senator Fulbright, Chairman of the Senate Foreign Relations Committee, who was responsible, in part, for the passage of the Tonkin Resolution in 1964, said in 1966:

> The Gulf of Tonkin incident was a very vague one. . . . We have no way of knowing, even to this day, what actually happened. I don't know whether we provoked that attack in connection with the supervising of help in a raid by South Vietnam or not.[11]

In our earlier discussion of the legality of U.S. intervention in Vietnam in relation to the right of individual and collective self-defense against armed attack, we saw that any resort to armed force in self-defense must be confined to those cases in which "the necessity of self-defense is instant, overwhelming and leaving no choice of means and no moment of deliberation."

In light of that limitation, it would appear that the Vietcong attack upon the United States garrison at Camp Holloway at Pleiku on February 7, 1965, which was essentially an attack by Vietcong guerrillas, was therefore a normal military activity during a civil war in which one side was being aided by an alien force. The raid was clearly a desperate effort to eliminate that force, and did not constitute the kind of attack which, under the United Nations Charter concept, is an armed attack of such an "overwhelming" character that "the necessity of self-defense is instant."

A judicious consideration of the Pleiku attack must result in the conclusion that the U.S. response to it came about not because there was "no moment of deliberation," but because that response was the final act of a well-organized, well-planned, and strategically conceived military campaign.

The term "aggression," set out at the beginning of this chapter, as proposed by the United States and five other members of the United Nations, is applicable "to the use of force in international relations, overt or covert, direct or indirect, by a State against the territorial integrity or political independence of any other State."

It would appear that the presence of 23,000 "advisers" and a "troop strength" of 18,000 men could, under the proposed definition of aggression, be considered an indirect if not actually a direct aggression on the part of the United States in Vietnam.

7:

The Song My Massacre and United States War Crimes in Vietnam

The incident at Song My came to public attention late in November 1969. It is alleged to have occurred on March 16, 1968. Why it took so long for so shocking an incident to come to public attention will be referred to later.

The bare facts are that Company C of the First Battalion of the 11th Brigade received written orders to leave for Song My. First Lieutenant William L. Calley, Jr., was in charge of the company. The written orders, as read to the troops while they were approaching Song My were "to destroy Pinkville [that was the Army reference to Song My] and everything in it." Varnado Simpson, one of the men who admitted that he had taken part in the killing, although with reluctance, said that he was following a direct order. Captain Ernest Medina had ordered his men "to go into the village and kill or burn down anything in sight."[1]

Paul David Meadlo, 22, a farm boy from Indiana, confessed that he personally killed thirty-five to forty civilians, and he put the total figure of civilians slain at Song My at about 370. Meadlo reported that he and First Lieutenant Calley, Jr., shot the civilians with their M-16 rifles. Meadlo and his parents appeared on a national hook-up on television. His mother, horrified at what her son confessed to, stated: "I sent them a good boy and they made him a murderer." Meadlo's father stated: "I would have shot the one who demanded me to do it." [2]

Sergeant Michael A. Bernhardt, who served in the platoon commanded by First Lieutenant Calley, Jr., stated: "The whole thing [at Song My] was so deliberate. It was point blank murder. . . .

"I walked up and saw these men doing strange things. They were doing it in three ways. One: They were setting fire to the hootches [dwellings] and huts and waiting for the people to come out and shooting them up. Two: They were going into the hootches and shooting them up. Three: They were gathering people in groups and shooting them.

"As I walked in you could see piles of people all through the village . . . all over. They were gathered up into large groups.

"I saw them shoot an M-79 [grenade launcher] into a group who were still alive. But it [the shooting] was mostly done with a machine gun. They were shooting women and children just like anybody else." [3]

One congressman who was shown the pictures taken of the Song My episode stated that "the pictures were pretty gruesome." Another congressman who left the private briefing before it ended stated: "That's why I walked out. I have one of those queasy stomachs." Yet another congressman, a former infantry captain in World War II, emerged from the showing equally shaken. "Having been in combat myself, I thought I would be hardened. But I must say I am a bit sickened." [4]

Newsweek summarized the Song My episode as follows: "And, indeed, the Song My affair—with its frightening implication that there might be still other, undisclosed atrocities buried in the U.S. Army's records—struck at America's moral and philosophical foundations. . . . To some Americans, the case stood as a horrible metaphor for the entire U.S. commitment in Vietnam." [5]

The massacre at Song My, horrible and shameful as it is, must not be seen as an isolated episode. In Chapter Two above are some excerpts from newspaper and magazine reports of atrocities that occurred in Vietnam during the years 1965–1967 inclusive.

The extent to which the Song My massacre has disturbed the thinking of governments throughout the world is, in a measure, revealed in a speech by the British Minister of Defense, Denis Healey, to the House of Commons on February 4, 1970, in which he stated that he was treating with "concern and urgency" accusations that British troops massacred twenty-five alleged terrorists in Malaya in 1948. It had been reported that on December 12, 1948, a battalion of Scots Guards shot and killed twenty-five Chinese plantation workers held prisoner as suspected terrorists. Because of the implications that flowed from the Song My massacre, Healey feared that Great Britain too might be charged with guilt comparable to that of Song My. Minister of Defense Healey was therefore calling for all available documents to decide whether to recommend a full criminal investigation.

The *New York Times* of February 5, 1970, reports that when the present Malaysian Government was asked for its views with regard to the massacre of December 12, 1948, its response was that it did not feel there was a comparison between the incident twenty-one years ago, on a rubber estate near Kuala Lumpur, and the alleged events in South Vietnam involving American troops.

. . .

First Lieutenant William L. Calley, Jr., was in charge of the platoon that carried out Captain Ernest Medina's orders "to destroy Pinkville [more specifically known as My Lai 4, a hamlet within the village of Song My] and everything in it." First Lieutenant Calley, Jr., has been charged with the premeditated murder of 109 civilians and will face a general court-martial.

On December 31, 1969, Staff Sergeant David Mitchell was charged with assault and intent to murder thirty Vietnamese civilians in connection with what happened at Song My on March 16, 1968, the day of the alleged massacre. He will face a general court-martial.

On or about January 8, 1970, Private Gerald Anthony Smith and Sergeant Charles E. Hutto were also charged with murder and other offenses in connection with the alleged killing of civilians in Song My on March 16, 1968.

According to *Newsweek,* "the harsh reality of Song My suddenly was etched in sharp and repugnant detail. True, it is still unclear precisely how many South Vietnamese civilians had fallen victim to American bullets. Figures ranged from 109 to 567. But the conclusion was that the killings at Song My shocked the American conscience." [6]

Careful research will reveal that the episode at Song My was horrible only because circumstances brought the episode to the attention of the American public, but others, no less shocking, preceded Song My and we might assume have been repeated since March 16, 1968.

On February 20, 1968, Tom Wicker in the *New York Times* reported that "Heavy bombs, aircraft rockets, naval gunfire, napalm, tear gas and all the usual ground weapons from eight-inch howitzers to tank guns are being used in heavily populated city areas."

On February 25, 1968, according to a Reuter's dispatch,

Hue was virtually destroyed by American troops, block by block, house by house.

The *New York Times* of January 11, 1967, reported the following episode which took place at the village of Ben Suc. Pacification in Ben Suc had been a total failure, so "the only military or political solution for the place," according to the colonel in charge, was resettlement. "I imagine there will be a lot of wailing and gnashing of teeth, but they will do what they are told," said the colonel. Some might not do what they are told, of course. "Forty-one villagers did not. During the day they were tracked down and killed. The conclusion? Soon the government will have no need to win the hearts and minds of Ben Suc. There will be no Ben Suc." [7]

A careful reading of the international conventions relating to the conduct of war—the Hague Convention of 1907, the Geneva Convention of 1949 with respect to the Protection of Civilians in Time of War and the Treatment of Prisoners of War, and the "Nuremberg Principles of International Law" (1946–1950)—*all indicate that the episodes at Song My, Ben Suc, Hue, and elsewhere are war crimes* as defined by the "Nuremberg Principles."

Professor Richard A. Falk of Princeton University has written two illuminating essays since the Song My massacre was exposed. One is entitled "War Crimes and Individual Responsibility: A Legal Memorandum." The other is "War Crimes—The Circle of Responsibility," published in *The Nation* on January 26, 1970. Both essays constitute scholarly treatment of the law anent the Song My massacre. (Professor R. A. Falk is editor of *The Vietnam War and International Law,* Vols. I and II, and in his capacity as Chairman of the Consultative Council of the Lawyers Committee on American Policy Towards Vietnam has directed the legal analysis of the Vietnam war in a book published by this committee—*Vietnam and International Law.**)

With Professor Falk's permission, the author will advert briefly to the source material contained in both essays, as well as to some of the conclusions arrived at by Professor Falk.

First Lieutenant William L. Calley, Jr., Staff Sergeant David Mitchell, Sergeant Charles E. Hutto, and Private Gerald Anthony Smith have all been charged with murder and are to be tried by a general court-martial.

It is the writer's view that under the "Nuremberg Principles of International Law," the charges of premeditated murder were lodged against these men only to give the United States Army jurisdiction over their offense under the Uniform Code of Military Justice.

It is the writer's further view that the general court-martial has no jurisdiction to try First Lieutenant Calley, Jr., and the other participants in the Song My atrocities because the superior officers in the Army are potential co-defendants under the "Nuremberg Principles."

The full text of the "Nuremberg Principles" appears in Appendix D. Principles III and IV read as follows:

> *Principle III*
>
> The fact that a person who committed an act which constitutes a crime under international law acted as Head of State or responsible government official does not relieve him from responsibility under international law.
>
> *Principle IV*
>
> The fact that a person acted pursuant to order of his Government or of a superior does not relieve him from

* Lawyers Committee on American Policy Towards Vietnam, *Vietnam and International Law* (Flanders: O'Hare Books, 1968).

> responsibility under international law, provided a moral choice was in fact possible to him.

The question is often asked to what extent are the countries of the world bound under the "Nuremberg Principles." Such a question is anticipated by the Clergy and Laymen Concerned About Vietnam in their book *In the Name of America* (page 43). Their introduction reads, in part:

> On December 11, 1946, the General Assembly of the United Nations unanimously affirmed "the principles of international law recognized by the Charter of the Nuremberg Tribunal and the judgment of the Tribunal." Subsequently, the General Assembly entrusted the formulation of the Nuremberg principles to the International Law Commission, an organ of the United Nations composed of experts in international law representing all the legal systems of the world and expected to promote the progressive development and codification of international law. It should be appreciated that the United States (together with France, Britain, and the Soviet Union) took a leading role in the drafting of the Nuremberg Charter, and in the prosecution of the German leaders that led to the Nuremberg judgment. . . .
>
> The approval of these principles by the General Assembly and their formulation by the International Law Commission, together with the participation of the United States Government in this process, makes these principles highly authoritative guides as to the character of relevant legal obligations of citizens and leaders.

The offenses committed by Lieutenant Calley and the other participants, as a matter of fact, constitute war crimes and should be tried by duly designated war crimes tribunals.

Captain Medina, who read the order directing the massacre at Song My, as yet has not been charged with a war crime. We then must follow the chain of command to determine who issued the orders to Captain Medina. The final result may well be that the decision to wipe out Song My was made by higher-ranking military men and responsible government officials.

Song My may have been a reprisal for the humiliating defeat suffered by the United States Army during the 1968 Tet offensive. The atrocities at Song My, it would appear, constitute a "war crime" on a par with Lidice. It will be recalled that Lidice, a village of some 500 inhabitants, was ordered to be wiped out as a reprisal for the slaying by Czech partisans of the Nazi Reichsprotector in Prague, Czechoslovakia. The S.S. (*Schutzstaffel*) at Lidice shot all the men, separated the children from their mothers, and shipped the women to concentration camps. At Song My, the company that was ordered to massacre all the living in that village did not even spare the women and children.

To be sure, "superior orders" are no defense in a prosecution for war crimes. By the same token, it would appear, under Principle III of the "Nuremberg Principles," that the fact that a person who committed acts which constitute war crimes acted as the Head of State or as a responsible government official at the time the acts were committed does not relieve him from responsibility under international law.

If the war crimes tribunal should not be able to reach the "Heads of State" or "responsible government officials," it may yet be able to reach the commanding officer who was in charge of the operation in Vietnam. This commanding officer could be held personally liable under the United States Supreme Court decision in the *Matter of Yamashita*.

In that case, the United States Supreme Court upheld a sentence of death pronounced on General Yamashita for acts committed by troops under his command in World

War II. Professor Falk, in his article "War Crimes—The Circle of Responsibility," makes the following observation on the significance of the Yamashita case:

> The following sentences from the majority opinion of Chief Justice Stone in the *Matter of Yamashita* have a particular bearing:
>
> > "It is evident that the conduct of military operations by troops whose excesses are unrestrained by the orders or efforts of their commanders would almost certainly result in violations which it is the purpose of the law of war to prevent. Its purpose to protect civilian populations and prisoners of war from brutality would largely be defeated if the commands of an invading army could with impunity neglect to take responsible measures for their protection. Hence the law of war presupposes that its violation is to be avoided through the control of the operation of war by commanders who are to some extent responsible for their subordinates." [327 U.S. 1, 15.]
>
> In fact, the effectiveness of the law of war depends, above all else, on holding those in command and in policy-making positions responsible for rank-and-file behavior on the field of battle.[8]

The conviction of General Yamashita by a war crimes tribunal, and the fact that the United States Supreme Court upheld that conviction, gives validity to the thesis that persons charged with the commission of war crimes should be tried by specially constituted war crimes tribunals rather than by general courts-martial.

Another instance supporting the thesis that war crimes should be tried by specially convened war crimes tribunals is that of the conviction of Admiral Erich Raeder by the Nuremberg Tribunal in October 1946. In April 1940, Germany launched an invasion of Norway. Admiral Raeder was charged with responsibility for having conducted that raid. He defended his action with the claim that word had been received that Great Britain was planning to invade Norway and that therefore the German invasion was justified by international law under the principle of anticipatory self-defense. The Nuremberg Tribunal rejected that defense and sentenced Admiral Erich Raeder to life imprisonment.*

The logic of Principle III of the "Nuremberg Principles" supports the thesis that "Heads of State" and "responsible government officials" are not immune from trial for acts which constitute war crimes.

A war crimes tribunal might very well find that the assault upon the camp at Pleiku on February 7, 1965, was not an "armed attack" of such enormity that it justified the bombardment of North Vietnam on February 7, 1965.† The decision to bombard North Vietnam might very well be considered an act by "responsible government officials" that could not be defended under Principle III of the "Nuremberg Principles."

Mr. Justice Robert H. Jackson, Chief Prosecutor for the United States at the Nuremberg Tribunal, had stated that "If certain acts in violation of treaties are crimes, they are crimes whether the United States does them or whether Germany does them, and we are not prepared to lay down a rule of criminal conduct against others which we would not be willing to have invoked against us."[9]

We are today, in light of the Song My revelations, bound to carry out Justice Jackson's commitment and agree to the appointment of a war crimes commission and a war crimes tribunal vested with authority to receive proof that the acts

---

* Appendix C, p. 4.

† See Chapter Five, subsection C.

of persons constitute war crimes because they are in violation of the law of war and with competence to render judgments of guilt or innocence of the persons so charged.

"The issue of responsibility is raised for all citizens who in various ways endorse the war policies of the government. The circle of responsibility is drawn around all who have or should have knowledge of the illegal and immoral character of the war." [10]

The general courts-martial that will sit in judgment of First Lieutenant William L. Calley, Jr., Staff Sergeant David Mitchell, Sergeant Charles E. Hutto, and Private Gerald Anthony Smith lack the competence to try them because the members of the general court-martial, or other army officers of comparable rank, may themselves be guilty of war crimes triable by war crimes commissions and war crimes tribunals.

The "circle of responsibility" Professor Falk adverted to is large enough to include not only persons who committed war crimes in the theater of war, but also persons whose decisions and acts were responsible for the involvement of the United States in a war that is in violation of international treaties and conventions.

The judgments of guilt of General Yamashita and Admiral Raeder would not have been imposed by a general court-martial. The guilt of the "Heads of State" at Nuremberg could not have been established by any tribunal other than the one created under the scope of the "Nuremberg Principles."

The general courts-martial now designated to try the Song My defendants should be declared as lacking in authority to try persons whose acts actually constituted war crimes. A special war crimes tribunal should be established to try *all* persons whose acts constitute war crimes.

The lack of competence of a general court-martial to try

persons for acts constituting war crimes is revealed by the manner in which the "military dragged their feet and their law books as long as they could. . . . Rumors of the massacre began to spread almost immediately, and the Brigade Commander, Col. Oren K. Henderson began an informal inquiry. In a series of informal interviews, he found no reason to believe that an atrocity had occurred, and it was not until a year later that a letter from Ronald Redenhour, a former American trooper who had heard eye-witness accounts of the slaughter, finally prompted a more thorough inquiry." [11]

President Richard M. Nixon did order a full investigation designed to determine whether U.S. commanders had tried to cover up the alleged massacre of Vietnamese civilians by U.S. troops. Lieutenant General William R. Peers headed the panel whose basic responsibility was "to determine whether there had been mass killings March 16, 1968, at the My Lai 4 hamlet of the Song My village complex, and whether such killings were hushed up."

On March 18, 1970, Lieutenant General Peers submitted his findings. The Army accused fourteen officers, two of whom were generals, of "dereliction of duty, failure to obey lawful regulations, and false swearing." General Peers stated at the Pentagon news conference that "Our inquiry clearly established that a tragedy of major proportions occurred there on that day. Whether trials by court-martial are warranted is to be determined." [12]

By way of defense and extenuation of Major General Samuel W. Koster, one of the two generals charged, it was observed that the disorganization that was incident to the Tet offensive brought on such demoralization that no commanding officer could be held accountable for the pressures that prevailed.[13]

. . .

Students of international law and constitutional law may urge that under our system of jurisprudence there is no provision for the establishment of a war crimes tribunal. Further, they may point out that the Nuremberg Charter, under which the Nazi war criminals were tried, provided for the trials of specific war crimes and their perpetration and that when those criminals were tried and convicted, the validity of the Nuremberg Charter terminated. If that estimate of the validity of the Nuremberg Charter should be accepted, then the United States Federal Courts should entertain the trial of acts which constitute war crimes and which are today being tried by general courts-martial under the Uniform Code of Military Justice.

United States Federal Courts have jurisdiction over issues concerning federal law, including the Constitution and treaties which are "the supreme law of the land."

In earlier chapters we considered the breaches by the United States of the United Nations Charter, the Geneva Accords of 1954, the SEATO Treaty, and the fact that our intervention in Vietnam constituted an act of aggression. We took the position that in Vietnam the United States was waging an "undeclared war" and that under the Tonkin Resolution our involvement was in effect an unconstitutional exercise of presidential power.

The United States is a party to all those treaties and they are, therefore, the "supreme law of the land." In addition to these treaties, the United States adheres to the provisions of the Hague Convention of 1907, the Kellogg-Briand Pact of 1928, and the Geneva Treaties of 1949.

The Vietnam war is being waged by indiscriminate coastal and aerial bombardment and "Free Zone" bombardment, search and destroy, as well as scorched earth programs that are in utter violation of the treaty provisions for the conduct of war.

The United States Federal Courts cannot evade their responsibility to punish acts of Americans that are in violation of treaties to which we are a party and which constitute the "supreme law of the land." Nor can the Supreme Court evade its responsibility by the excuse that under the doctrine of the separation of powers, questions concerning the initiation and conduct of hostilities are usually "political questions" in which it, the Supreme Court, must follow the political organs of the government, Congress and the Executive.

The Supreme Court must direct that the provisions of the treaties be enforced in every instance in which those treaties are breached by United States military personnel or "responsible government officials." Breaches of these treaties should not be left for adjudication by general courts-martial pursuant to the Uniform Code of Military Justice. A court-martial, unlike a civilian jury, is not chosen at random from the community, but by the commander or his subordinates.

A recent Supreme Court decision held that "a Court-Martial is not yet an independent instrument of justice, but remains, to a significant degree, a specialised part of the over-all mechanism by which military discipline is preserved." [14]

The true character of a court-martial decision was revealed in the recent case of First Lieutenant James B. Duffy. First Lieutenant Duffy was tried and convicted of the premeditated murder of a Vietnamese farmer captured during an ambush patrol. The court-martial trying First Lieutenant Duffy was made up of eight Army officers. They found First Lieutenant Duffy guilty as charged. But when the officers of the court-martial were informed that the verdict which they rendered carried a mandatory sentence of life imprisonment, they asked for leave to reconsider their verdict and, over objection of the prosecutor, entered a new verdict of guilty of negligent homicide and imposed a sentence of only six months confinement.

The decision in the Duffy case gives some indication of what we might expect in the court-martial trials of the Song My defendants if they remain in the hands of the general court-martial.

Professor Edward F. Sherman, in his study of the Duffy case, states, in part, "Military law permits a court to reconsider its verdict, a practice remaining from the day when commanders could refuse to accept a court's verdict which was not to their liking and require it to reconsider.[15]

The virtual exoneration of First Lieutenant Duffy impelled an Army law officer to observe: "To a lot of us it looks like another example of the M.G.R.—the 'Mere Gook Rule.' "[16]

If the administration of Army justice will be governed by the doctrine of "Mere Gook Rule" then the administration of justice by general court-martial will be justly scorned and held in contempt.*

---

* It was reported in the *New York Times* on June 24, 1970, after this chapter was written, that two Army officers who had been charged with covering up the Song My episode had been exonerated.

The Army dismissed criminal charges against Brigadier General George H. Young, Jr., and Colonel Nels A. Parsons, who had been accused of "failure to obey lawful regulations and dereliction of duty." This exoneration of officers without trial highlights, once again, the Army's refusal to adhere to the Nuremberg Principles, which point the finger at the ultimate culpability of officers in war crimes.

8:

"Endless War" and the Military-Industrial Complex

It seems that notable utterances in the area of political science are made by Presidents in their farewell addresses. It must be that the imminence of release from the responsibility of a decision-making office makes possible the statements of greatest truths.

President George Washington, in his farewell address of 1798, warned his countrymen against entering into entangling alliances in order to maintain peace.

President Dwight D. Eisenhower, in January 1961, on the eve of his departure from office, delivered what must be regarded as his most significant statement as President of the United States. As Commander of the Allied Forces during World War II, and later as President between 1952 and 1960, he experienced the full force of that formidable alliance in our country between the industrial captains and the military combine.

As World War II ended, the industrial magnates had amassed the gargantuan fortune of more than $300 billion, and the military force in our land had grown from a total of 428,000 officers and enlisted men in the Army and Navy in

1940 to an active armed force of over 3,400,000 men and women, with an additional 1,600,000 military reserves and National Guardsmen.

The most quoted words in President Eisenhower's farewell address are:

> In the councils of government, we must guard against the acquisition of unwarranted influence, whether sought or unsought, by the military-industrial complex. The potential for the disastrous rise of misplaced power exists and will persist.

General David M. Shoup, Commandant of the United States Marine Corps for four years before his retirement in December 1963, in his article "The New American Militarism," which appeared in the April 1969 issue of the *Atlantic,* gives us a thoroughly informed understanding of what the present American military giant actually is. In addition to our nearly five million military men and National Guardsmen, General Shoup points out:

> We are now a nation of veterans. To the 14.9 million veterans of World War II, Korea added another 5.7 million five years later, and ever since, the large peacetime military establishment has been training and releasing draftees, enlistees, and short-term reservists by the hundreds of thousands each year. In 1968 the total living veterans of U.S. military service numbered over 23 million, or about 20 percent of the adult population.

The general also reveals that in addition to the four services—Army, Navy, Air Force, and Marines—each of the four has its own association; and that there are also additional military functions, associations for ordinance, management, defense, industry, and defense transportation.

Senator George McGovern said, in an address before Yeshiva University in New York City on December 8, 1968:

> Mr. Nixon takes office with a military budget of more than $82 billion in the current year—$40 billion above the budget that led to President Eisenhower's warning eight years ago. The $82 billion now being spent directly on military items represents 56 percent of the total federal budget. This does not include such war-related expenditures as veterans' affairs and the interest on our war debts which would raise the total to $107 billion, or 72 percent of the federal budget. . . . Yet in the recent campaign Mr. Nixon spoke of the need to increase military and space outlays including the deployment of a costly anti-ballistic missile system and other new weapons—while reducing non-military portions of the budget. One can hear in Washington these days from well-informed sources that even if the war in Vietnam is ended, the military budget will climb to over $100 billion in the next four years. Certainly, both the cost and the influence of the military complex will continue to mount unless the new administration and the Congress exercise more prudence than we have seen in the past.

The extent to which the military-industrial complex is reassured of its tenure in our national, political, and economic picture is indicated in an observation by Mr. Edward LeFevre, who heads the Washington office of General Dynamics, the nation's largest arms contractor. As quoted by Senator McGovern, Mr. LeFevre put it this way: "Basically, we're a big systems builder for military weapons. Over 90 percent of our business is military. We're in that business to stay."

General Dynamics is perhaps one of the best situated and most favored builders of military hardware and, strangely enough, one of the least efficient of the "recognized" Pentagon favorites. General Dynamics had the sad experience of having thirteen of its F-11B planes crash in their twenty-six months of operation—yet in spite of this, General Dynamics is presently in line for the much-contested ABM (Anti-Ballistic Missile) and AMSA (Advance Manned Strategic Aircraft) contracts. General Dynamics' success in securing such prime contracts for the construction of the ABM and AMSA must be due in part to Deputy Defense Secretary David Packard's former directorship of General Dynamics until his Pentagon appointment.

Gordon W. Rule, a civilian procurement officer who was responsible for the F-11B aircraft, said, in testimony before the House Committee on Military Operations, that General Dynamics was in default on its contract because the planes were too heavy to meet the height or range requirements. Mr. Rule proposed, in a memorandum to Deputy Secretary of State Paul H. Nitze, that the contract be terminated for default. At the same time, Assistant Secretary of the Air Force Robert A. Charles and Roger Lewis, the chairman of General Dynamics, proposed that the Navy reimburse the company for all costs and impose no penalty. Nitze's compromise—save the mark—was to reimburse $216.5 million, mostly to General Dynamics, and to impose a small penalty.

In a later memorandum Mr. Rule commented on the attitude of defense contractors: "No matter how poor the quality, how late the product and how high the cost, they know nothing will happen to them." [1]

The defense industries, according to an article by Richard Kaufman in the *New York Times Magazine,* are perhaps the most highly subsidized industries in the nation's history.[2] It may therefore be understandable why the defense industries would prefer to have Vietnam and future Vietnams continue indefinitely. Not only are these industries subsidized by the United States Treasury, but the suppliers of military hardware need not be concerned about competition. The rule affecting exceptions can easily be invoked to make a supplier of materials to the Pentagon completely without competition of any kind.

It appears further that the defense industry, in addition to providing high profits for low risks, offers fringe benefits for everyone. One of the important advantages for those in procurement on either side of the bargaining table is the opportunity for career advancement. There is a steady march of military and civilian personnel back and forth between the Pentagon and defense industries.

Litton Industries, one of the most formidable conglomerates in the United States, according to *Fortune* magazine's list of the five hundred largest industrial companies, finds itself in fortieth place among the five hundred. In 1967, Litton was thirty-sixth on the list of prime defense contractors, but in 1968 it had advanced to fourteenth on the list. According to Senator William Proxmire's discussion of the thousands of military officers who secure employment with the Pentagon contractors (*Congressional Record* of May 5, 1967), former Assistant Secretary of Defense Thomas Morris went directly from his position as chief Pentagon procurement officer to a top job with Litton. The Senator considers Morris' employment by Litton Industries "more serious than the hiring of Admirals and Generals by defense contractors. Morris has been the big boss of all military procurement." Senator Proxmire further pointed out that 90 percent of defense contracting is not by competitive bidding but by some form of negotiation. Certainly Thomas Morris could be useful in guiding the Litton team that undertakes to secure Pentagon business. And he would have considerable help, since Litton has at least forty-nine retired military officers above the rank of colonel or the equivalent on its payroll, not counting those on its Board of Directors who have been army officers—for example, General Carl A. Spaatz, John H. Rubel, etc. David Packard, Assistant Secretary of Defense, is a former senior vice-president of the company.

The threat of the military-industrial complex lies in its enormous influence. It is reasonable to assume that a war machine is a necessary evil. What is alarming is the size of the machine, as shown not only through its influence on the giant companies, but also through its wide influence nationally in maintaining small industries where unskilled labor is employed at salaries equal to those of highly skilled labor in peacetime operations.

The distribution of war contracts among small subcontractors throughout the country has an effect on attitudes toward the Vietnam war. People in small communities which are beneficiaries of the largess of subcontracting military procurement contracts would quite naturally be concerned about any threat to their local industry.

> The military-industrial complex is becoming a massive tangled system half inside and half outside the government. Like the Gordian Knot, it is too intricate to be unravelled, but, like the dinosaur, its weakness lies in its great size. If its intricacy rebuffs us, its grossness is vulnerable; it can be reduced by substantially cutting the defense budget.[3]

The complex has its tentacles deep in our political structure. In an article entitled "The War Machine Under Nixon," I. F. Stone indicates that in 1966 the Armed Services Committees of both Houses recommended extra funds to speed the projects referred to as "the two plums" the military-industrial complex most wanted on the eve of the 1968 campaign—the ABM and the AMSA.

Defense Secretary McNamara, however, refused to spend these appropriations, and President Johnson then made two moves that cleared the way for both projects. First, in September 1967, Johnson persuaded McNamara to agree to a "thin" ABM system, a military undertaking in which Secretary of Defense McNamara clearly had no interest. Two months later, Stone goes on to say, "Johnson made the surprise announcement—as much a surprise to McNamara as to the press—that he was shifting the redoubtable Pentagon chief to the World Bank." That cleared the way for ABM and AMSA too. It also cleared the way for the 1968 campaign.[4]

Johnson's maneuvers may not have been completely unrelated to the needs of political candidates. In recent decades costs of presidential campaigns have run into millions of dollars. The military-industrial complex has been acknowledged as the readiest source of campaign funds and political support for the nomination and the election of Presidents. It has been observed by astute readers of the political scene that it is a most skillfully hidden source, and that the escalations in military expenditures which followed the 1960 and 1968 presidential campaigns were not totally unrelated to the influence of the military-industrial complex.

An article in the Washington *Post* by Bernard Nossiter, analyzing the role of major military contractors (quoted by Senator George McGovern in his address at Yeshiva on December 8, 1968), says flatly:

> The companies are understandably guarded in talking about the effects of more immediate political changes on

> their future. But they leave little doubt that an important source of their optimism lies in the departure of Defense Secretary Robert McNamara and the election of Richard Nixon.

"People are pressing for new programs more intensely than ever," said W. Paul Thayer, the ex-test pilot who runs Ling's L.T.V. Aerospace. "With McNamara stepping out, that was the turning point."

The plans of the military-industrial complex for military needs beyond Vietnam are illuminated in I. F. Stone's *New York Review of Books* article referred to above. Stone observes that, while there was a $3.5 billion reduction in the 1970 Vietnam war budget, that reduction was not made available to the starved civilian and welfare services of the United States, but rather for the following purposes, as quoted from page 74 of the Budget of the United States Government for Fiscal 1970:

> As shown in the accompanying table, outlays in support of Southeast Asia are anticipated to drop for the first time in 1970—declining by $3.5 billion from 1969. This decline reflects changing patterns of combat activity and revised loss projections. *Outlays for* the military activities of the Department of Defense, excluding support of Southeast Asia, are expected to rise by $4.1 billion in 1970, to provide selected force improvements. [Emphasis added.] [5]

What is indicated above is the background of the stalemate that the United States people find themselves in now: the Vietnam war has been grinding away for more than four years. The almost complete Americanization of that war has increasingly revealed it as a conflict between a U.S.A. Goliath and an N.L.F. David.

The Paris peace negotiations are still fruitless after more

than a year of discussion. And President Nixon, to appease the voices at home demanding an end to the war, has declared that the United States will withdraw a very few of its troops. Clearly President Nixon's speeches on the subject are not clarion calls to bring the war to an end.

Today there are two schools of thought on the issues of terminating the war. One school is of the opinion that the Johnson "blunder" and "miscalculation" in Vietnam must be corrected as soon as it can conveniently be done. General David M. Shoup, in his article in the *Atlantic,* pointed out:

> We maintain more than 1,517,000 Americans in uniform overseas in 119 countries. We have eight treaties to help defend 48 nations if they ask us to—or if we choose to intervene in their affairs.
>
> For years up to 1964 the chiefs of the armed services, of whom the author was then one, deemed it unnecessary and unwise for U.S. forces to become involved in any ground war in Southeast Asia. In 1964 there were changes in the composition of the Joint Chiefs of Staff, and in a matter of a few months the Johnson Administration, encouraged by the aggressive military, hastened into what has become the quagmire of Vietnam. The intention at the time was that the war effort be kept small and "limited."

Almost five years of resistance to *Schrecklichkeit* by the Vietnamese have persuaded many influential Americans that the war should be ended as quickly as possible. This may not be quite in keeping with the program laid down by Henry Kissinger, the President's Adviser on National Security. In his article in *Foreign Affairs* of January 1969, "The Vietnam Negotiations," he observed that a coalition government was undesirable. Mr. Kissinger wrote:

> The issue is whether the United States should be a party to the attempt to *impose* a coalition government. We must

> be clear that our involvement in such an effort may well destroy the existing political structure of Vietnam and thus lead to a communist take-over. . . .
>
> In short, negotiations seeking to impose a coalition from the outside arc likely to change markedly and irreversibly the political process in South Vietnam—as Vietnamese who believe that a coalition government cannot work quickly choose sides. We would, in fact, be settling the war on an issue least amenable to outside influence, with respect to which we have the least grasp of conditions, and the long-term implications of which are the most problematical.

The school of thought that believes an early peace is desirable adopts the premise that Wall Street, the multinational corporations, the foundation technocrats, the major news media, and the international bankers all still consider the Vietnam intervention to have been essentially correct, but the tenacity of the Vietnamese resistance disastrously underestimated. They believe the military and its civilian spokesmen sold them a bill of goods whose cost has become unbearably high. The enterprise has got to be liquidated. It remains to be seen whether Pentagon pressure can hold out for long against this growing pessimism and doubt.

Another school of thought believes that as long as our posture in Vietnam was that of adviser and helper, it could have been claimed (quite correctly) that the South Vietnam regime had shown itself incapable of using U.S. advice, and that this released the United States from all further obligations to it; but that once the war was Americanized the undertaking underwent a qualitative change. It was no longer a weak and shaky government of a backward half-country against the Communists, but the mighty, all-powerful United States of America against the forces of a country with about 15 percent of the population of the United States and an infinitesimal percentage of the per capita income.

The conclusion of this school of thought is that:

> For the United States to admit defeat under these circumstances—and we should be clear that withdrawal from Vietnam would be precisely that—would entail a loss of face on a scale the world has probably never seen before. The Chinese contention that the United States is a paper tiger would be proved to the hilt, and every radical and revolutionary movement around the world would be encouraged to believe that what had been accomplished in Vietnam could, sooner or later, be duplicated everywhere else. Much as the elders might want to liquidate the war, they could only contemplate consequences of this sort with extreme misgivings and consternation.[6]

The military-industrial complex is still as formidable as it ever was, if not really more so. It is looking ahead to the possibility of the termination of the Vietnam war. To the complex, however, this termination is only the end of one campaign in its endless war of containment of communism in every area of the globe. The "selected force improvements" in the 1970 military budget are to be used in this war.

The stalemate following the Korean war, a war which the United States hardly claims as a victory, left Korea divided. An American force of 55,000 men has remained there since 1954. Since the end of World War II the French, British, and Dutch forces have departed from Asia. The United States, especially since the Geneva Accords of 1954, has been unilaterally attempting to fill the "vacuum" left by the former colonial powers in that part of the world. One of the consequences of this policy for the American people seems to be an endless war in Vietnam with prospects of its continuation in Thailand or Indonesia or Korea.

The military-industrial complex is geared to an endless war. The appropriations made available to the Pentagon to perpetuate this unholy alliance of ambitious military men and conscienceless war-profiteers enable it to make virtual prisoners of the American people.

9:

Total Withdrawal: The Only Solution

Chapter Two described the "escalation of resistance" to the war that is asserting itself at home. Civilian awareness of the illegality of our presence in Vietnam, and the determination to translate it into action, expressed themselves most clearly in the declaration of college students at graduation ceremonies in June 1969 that they would prefer prison to service in the Vietnam war.

Only two months later, on August 26, 1969, the front pages of almost all newspapers in the country carried a report from Vietnam captioned "Sir, My Men Refuse to Go!" It appeared that the Alpha Company of the 196th Light Infantry Brigade was ordered to move down a jungle slope and refused to obey its commander. The men persisted in their mutinous conduct even though they were told "what it means to disobey orders under fire."

In every American war there have been isolated incidents of mutiny among troops. As James Reston wrote in the *New York Times,* "There is a breaking point where discipline, duty and even loyalty to the men at your side are overwhelmed by fear and death and a paralyzing feeling of the senselessness of the whole bloody operation. And we are now getting a glimpse of it in Vietnam." [1]

Newsweek flew a correspondent to Da Nang to ascertain what lay behind the mutinous conduct of Alpha Company. His account said:

> As in no other modern U.S. war there is a malaise among the troops in Vietnam. Hatred for the war runs deep, especially among the young draftees. As more and more younger soldiers arrive from the United States, the anti-war spirit mounts. And at a time when the administration seems bent, however cautiously, on withdrawal from Vietnam, the soldier inevitably asks himself why he should risk his neck in a war nobody wants to win.[2]

Disillusionment about the war was not limited to the men in Company A. Even before the incident, a *New York Times* correspondent had reported:

> Conversations with scores of infantrymen throughout [Vietnam] over the last several months have produced such answers as "I fight because that's the only way to stay alive out here. . . . I don't believe the war is necessary. I just work hard at surviving so I can go home and protest all this killing." [3]

While this disillusionment and revolt against the war is accelerating, President Nixon's diplomacy is becoming more difficult to understand, if it is not actually a paradox. While in Vietnam in early August, President Nixon told a group of U.S. soldiers about to set off on patrol that the Vietnam war might sometime be regarded as "one of America's finest hours." [4]

Before starting his round-the-world tour, President Nixon had announced the withdrawal of 25,000 troops from Vietnam, to reduce American commitments around the world and prevent "future Vietnams." During his stay in Bangkok, the President "promised to stand with Thailand against those who might threaten it from abroad or from within." Senator Gore of the Foreign Relations Committee immediately rejected the President's Bangkok speech as constituting "a military commitment which the President had no authority to make," and as "a statement of policy threatening more Vietnams." [5]

Nixon's statement of commitment to Thailand resurrected a conflict between the President and Senator Fulbright, the Chairman of the Senate Foreign Relations Committee, as to how deeply we are committed to Thailand under the SEATO agreement. This conflict led to the Senate's discovery of a military "contingency plan" under which U.S. military personnel would come under the command of the Thailand General Staff—a rather unique, if not highly embarrassing, situation.

The extent to which the United States is involved in Southeast Asia is revealed by a Washington dispatch which appeared on the front page of the *New York Times* on December 1, 1969. The story is captioned: "U.S. Costs to Get Thais to Join War Put at $1 Billion—Deal Is Reported to Include Equipment and Pay for Division in Vietnam—Program Began in 1966—Bangkok's List of Military Needs Is Said to Include Missiles and Jets."

It may well be that President Nixon will consider U.S. commitment to Thailand under the SEATO agreement to be even more binding than our commitment to Vietnam, since Thailand is a signatory to the SEATO agreement. Should that be so, United States involvement in that country will be even more ominous.

The discussion in Chapter Five of the illegality of our

presence in Vietnam under the SEATO agreement applies with equal validity, of course, to any involvement in support of Thailand.

The threat of involvement in Thailand is serious. On August 18, 1969, Secretary of State William P. Rogers sent a message to Bangkok stating that the United States "will honor its commitment to Thailand as embodied in the SEATO Treaty." [6] Secretary Rogers' message was preceded by a statement from Senator Charles H. Percy of Illinois, who predicted, during a meeting with the Thai Foreign Minister, that only a token 1,500 U.S. servicemen would be withdrawn from Thailand, out of the approximately 50,000 U.S. servicemen who have been stationed there for some years.[7]

The "honorable peace" that President Nixon is making a condition for the termination of hostilities in Vietnam does not differ from the conditions formulated by President Johnson during the closing days of his administration. In essence, the coin of the realm during the closing days of the first year of the Nixon administration was a piece of currency with two "heads," each side proclaiming continued military involvement on the Asian continent.

Before President Nixon announced the new policy of de-escalation, commencing with an initial withdrawal of 25,000 men from Vietnam, a Paris dispatch to *Newsweek* by Stewart Alsop observed that during the President's visit to Paris one of his chief policy advisers had an exchange of views with a high official of the French Government. The essence of the exchange was as follows:

> American Adviser: As you know, the President very much wants peace in Vietnam. But we feel that General deGaulle ought to understand two things. First, we cannot

withdraw American forces without any withdrawal by the other side. Second, we cannot sacrifice the Saigon government.

French Official: Then the President cannot have peace.[8]

On the question of reciprocal withdrawal of American forces and North Vietnam forces, it must be observed that the call for mutual withdrawal of foreign troops is predicated upon the dubious premise that the North Vietnamese and the Americans are equally foreign to Vietnam.

The position of the N.L.F. at the April 16, 1969, Paris talks is reported to have been the following: Delegate Tran Buu Kiem posed the position of his delegation on the question of reciprocity to the effect that the formula for mutual withdrawal of troops is an absolutely unreasonable demand because

> It places the aggressor and the victim fighting against this aggression on the same footing. . . . Logically, the United States, having illegally introduced troops of aggression against the South Vietnamese, trampling the national rights of the South Vietnamese people under foot, must naturally withdraw its troops without posing any conditions whatsoever.[9]

In discussing the difficulties which Henry Cabot Lodge, the American delegate to the Paris Peace Conference, was encountering, Mr. Alsop further observed that the United States' bargaining position at the Conference "would be improved by a marked deterioration of the Communist military position in Vietnam or by sharply increased military pressure by our side, or by both. But neither seems at all likely." Mr. Alsop concludes his dispatch as follows:

> President Nixon may, even so, have no choice but to begin withdrawing American troops. For the basic weak-

> ness in Cabot Lodge's bargaining position here lies in the simple fact that the American people have lost stomach for the war in Vietnam, and the Communists know it. People who have lost stomach for a war in the end generally lose the war. If that happens, it will be interesting, if perhaps a bit frightening, to see how the American people react to their first lost war.

Nothing has made more of an impact on the American people than the reports from the war zone which daily assault our senses, our conscience, and our attitudes.

The complete encirclement of a Marine contingent at Khe Sanh, a bastion which was ultimately abandoned, was followed by a later encirclement of a contingent of American Green Berets and artillerymen in an outpost at Ben Het; and, more recently, the complete encirclement of Hamburger Hill, a defeat for American military contingents that is not easily forgotten by the American people.

If the new policy of de-escalation in stages looks toward an ultimate division of Vietnam comparable to that which took place in Korea after 1953, then, indeed, the loss of almost 45,000 troops and nonfatal casualties of more than 280,000 will have been futile.

The question of withdrawal from Vietnam is not new to American diplomats. In earlier chapters we referred to the appearances of Secretary of State Rusk, General Gavin, former Ambassador Kennan, and General Taylor before the Senate Foreign Relations Committee on January 28, 1966, and February 4 to 18, 1966. It will be recalled that during his appearance General Gavin, who at one time served as Chief of Plans and Operations in the Department of the Army, stated, "It isn't vital for the future of the United States that we stay there. It isn't absolutely essential to our survival or to our future security that we stay there."[10]

Later Senator Lausche asked General Gavin:

> . . . The President of the United States has suggested that there be open and free elections in South Vietnam for the people of South Vietnam to determine at those elections what type of government they want. This morning I believe you said they ought to have that right, and if they chose a communist government, they should be permitted to have it. Is that correct?
>
> *Gen. Gavin:* That is what I said. I said they should have a government they chose. If it is the kind of government they like, fine. If it isn't, that is their choosing.[11]

Ambassador Kennan, during his appearance before the Committee on February 10, was questioned by Senator Morse:

> *Morse:* If the people of a country decide to vote themselves a communist regime or decide that they are willing to support a communist regime, do you think it is wise policy for the United States to use its great power to prevent those elections, or to intervene to prevent those people from having the kind of government that they want?
>
> *Kennan:* No, Senator. I don't. I don't think it was a wise policy. I recognize that this could create, depending on the place where it would happen, very difficult problems for our government. But it seems to me that, as people who profess to believe in the democratic process, we are in a poor position to object to the consequences of any free expression of opinion on the part of a people elsewhere in the world.[12]

On the question of U.S. commitment to the Saigon regime, Ambassador Kennan made the following observation in his formal statement to the Committee:

> And finally, when I hear it said that to adopt a defensive strategy in South Vietnam would be to rat on our commitment to the government of that territory, I am a little bewildered. I would like to know what that commitment really consists of and how and when it was incurred. What seems to be involved here is an obligation on our part not only to defend the frontiers of a certain political entity against outside attack, but to ensure the internal security of its government in circumstances where that government is unable to assure that security by its own means. Now, any such obligation is one that goes obviously considerably further in its implications than the normal obligation of a military alliance.[13]

Former Secretary of Defense Clark Clifford, in his article entitled "A Viet Nam Reappraisal," undertook to explain his rationale for disengagement in Vietnam. He had been exposed to the conflicting and paradoxical foreign policy positions of the closing days of the Johnson administration, which were also the final days of his service as Secretary of Defense. He wrote:

> As Saigon authorities saw it, the longer the war went on, with the large-scale American involvement, the more stable was their regime, and the fewer concessions they would have to make to other political groupings. . . . In short, grim and distasteful though it might be, I concluded during the bleak winter weeks that Saigon was in no hurry for the fighting to end and that the Saigon regime did not want us to reach an early settlement of military issues with Hanoi.[14]

Secretary Clifford came to the conclusion that "sooner or later, the test must be whether the South Vietnamese will serve their own country sufficiently well to guarantee its national survival. In my view, this test must be made sooner, rather than later." [15]

It was Clifford's view that a withdrawal of 100,000 troops should be made in 1969, and that "we should also make it clear that this is not an isolated action, but the beginning of a process under which all U.S. ground combat forces will have been withdrawn from Viet Nam by the end of 1970." [16]

President Nixon, in his press conference following the publication of Clifford's article, observed that he perhaps would do better than the troop withdrawal the former Secretary had suggested.

The fact is that in the late fall of 1969 President Nixon still did not appear to be taking measures to fulfill his commitment of withdrawal. A more justified conclusion is that the President, on his second round-the-world trip, visited the SEATO Treaty "allies" in Southeast Asia to reassure them that his policy is one of "moderate de-escalation."

In his concluding paragraphs, Secretary Clifford almost anticipated President Nixon's trip to the Near East, and he made this significant observation:

> In the long run, the security of the Pacific region will depend upon the ability of the countries there to meet the legitimate growing demands of their own people. No military strength we can bring to bear can give them internal stability or popular acceptance. In Southeast Asia, and elsewhere in the less developed regions of the world, our ability to understand and to control the basic forces that are at play is a very limited one. We can advise, we can urge, we can furnish economic aid. But American military power cannot build nations, any more than it can solve the social and economic problems that face us here at home.[17]

It would seem that the problem the Nixon administration and the American people face today is not whether de-escalation is the best solution to our involvement in Vietnam, but that, if ultimate withdrawal is not our policy, then there is only one alternative left—escalate the war, use the nuclear weapon, destroy Vietnam and destroy the tradition of the American people, in our effort to solve an insoluble situation.

There is yet another reason why we should withdraw from Vietnam and permit the Vietnamese to determine their own form of government after the conflict between the different regions comes to an end.

In Chapter Two we cited evidence of the way the war is being fought in Vietnam. The American role, as revealed in the dispatches quoted from *In the Name of America,* is not one our young men who are fighting in Vietnam are necessarily proud of. Letters sent to parents and wives reveal the utter humiliation of men fighting for a cause they cannot understand.

The young students at the universities, as indicated in the same chapter, also seem to understand that the war in Vietnam is not their war. Student leaders and editors of college newspapers have stated emphatically to President Nixon that they "cannot participate in a war which we consider to be immoral and unjust. We will not serve in the military as long as the war in Vietnam continues." The secretary of the senior class at Yale has stated that 143 members of the graduating class signed a petition indicating that "if confronted with the draft they would refuse induction, thereby risking jail sentences and jeopardizing careers to oppose the war"; and the student leaders' petition to the President also stated emphatically that they would prefer prison to service in Vietnam. They all speak for the conscience of American youth.

Today, resistance to the war continues to escalate. High school students have shown that they too have serious misgivings about service in the Vietnam war. And the possibility increases that the young draftees will also "lose stomach for the war in Vietnam" and refuse to serve in a war in which the security of the American people is not at stake. There is the further possibility that draftees in all walks of life will emulate the college students and choose prison terms over war service. During the coming year, unless it appears clear to the youth of America that the policy of our country is to withdraw from Vietnam, and not merely to de-escalate, the conflict at home on the issue of our presence in Vietnam will become more acute.

The resolution of the Vietnam war will not be found in a policy of de-escalation which contemplates a supervised election while American forces are still present in Vietnam. Nor will it be found in a policy that envisages the permanent stationing of a force comparable to the 55,000 troops that have been stationed in Korea since 1953.

The conflict in Vietnam is basically a civil war that has been in progress for more than twenty years. The French withdrew in 1954 after suffering a humiliating defeat at Dienbienphu. The United States forces should be withdrawn immediately and the Vietnamese people should be permitted to terminate their civil war and thereafter choose their own form of government.

After the invasion of Cambodia, two distinguished and perhaps the best informed diplomats on conditions in South Vietnam, one an American and the other a Frenchman, warned that only a complete withdrawal of United States forces from Indochina would bring peace to that part of the world.

Clark Clifford, adviser to Presidents Truman, Kennedy, and Johnson, who served as Secretary of Defense during the closing days of the Johnson administration, after rejecting the "domino" and the "blood bath" theories as reasons for remaining in Vietnam, stated that we "announce publicly that *all* [emphasis applied] United States military personnel would be out of Indochina by the end of 1971, at the latest, provided only that arrangements have been made for the release of United States prisoners of war." [18]

President Georges Pompidou of France, Premier during de Gaulle's presidency and high in government councils throughout the post-war French occupation of Indochina, stated at a news conference at the Elysée Palace, "that there will be no prospects for peace in Indochina until the day when the United States has taken, by itself, and voluntarily, the firm resolution to *vacate* [emphasis added] Indochina. That is the basis for everything. . . ." [19]

No two diplomats in either the United States or France were closer to the inner workings of diplomacy and military acts than Clark Clifford and Georges Pompidou. Their judgment should be persuasive in determining policy that will bring peace to that part of the world.

10:

The Cambodian Invasion: An Invitation to Disaster

On April 30, 1970, President Nixon informed the American people that in order to "avoid a wider war" and "keep casualties of our brave men in Vietnam at an absolute minimum" he had ordered American troops to invade Cambodia.

The manner in which President Nixon arrived at his decision, on careful analysis, was foreboding. Secretary of Defense Melvin Laird and Secretary of State William P. Rogers did not learn of the President's actual intentions until twenty-four hours before President Nixon went on the air, although the President admitted that his decision to invade Cambodia was made "two weeks ago." President Nixon in this instance acted "in effect as his own Secretary of State and Secretary of Defense." [1]

When Secretary of State Rogers appeared before a Congressional Committee on April 23, 1970, only one week before the order to invade was given, the Secretary of State declared: "We have no incentive to escalate. Our whole incentive is to de-escalate. We recognize that if we escalate and get involved in Cambodia with our ground troops, that our whole program [Vietnamization] is defeated."[2]

Friendly congressmen and senators were not only left in ignorance, but having been briefed by an out-of-touch Secretary of State, had a right to feel almost deceived. Secretary of Defense Melvin Laird was uninformed about the number of subsequent bombing raids on North Vietnam; the Secretary of State did not know about the raids at all.[3]

The *New York Times* responded to the Cambodia invasion as follows:

> President Nixon's assurance in his address last night that his decision to send American troops against Communist sanctuaries in Cambodia will save lives, hasten the withdrawal of American forces and shorten the war has a familiar and wholly unconvincing ring. . . .
>
> If reports from Pnompenh that the attack was launched without consultation with the Cambodian Government are true, the strike is a clear breach of Cambodian neutrality, the Geneva Accords and the principles of international law which the Administration has repeatedly cited in connection with the long-known and equally illegal Communist Vietnamese presence on Cambodian soil. . . .
>
> In sending American troops into Cambodia, President Nixon has rejected his own Nixon Doctrine in Southeast Asia, escalating a war from which he had promised to disengage. This is not the "new" Nixon who campaigned on a platform pledged to peace. It is more like the old Nixon who as Vice President in 1954 said the United States would have to send troops into Indochina if there were no other ways to prevent its fall to the Communists, then on the verge of defeating the French.[4]

In his June 3, 1970, address to the American people, President Nixon stated: "You will recall that on April 20, I announced the withdrawal of an additional 150,000 American troops from Vietnam within a year, which will bring the total number of withdrawals since I have taken office to 260,000. I also affirmed on that occasion our proposals for a negotiated peace." [5]

Clark Clifford declared the following:

> Like most Americans, I applauded the President's action in withdrawing 115,000 of our troops so far, and have noted his intention, with some qualifications, to withdraw 150,000 more in the next 12 months. . . . However, I cannot remain silent in the face of his reckless decision to send troops to Cambodia, continuing a course of action which I believe to be dangerous to the welfare of our nation. It is my opinion that President Nixon is taking our nation down a road that is leading us more deeply into Vietnam rather than taking us out.[6]

What pressures and influences had been brought to bear between April 20, when President Nixon decided to withdraw another 150,000 troops, and April 30, 1970, when he decided to dispatch a new military force to invade Cambodia, we may never know. Only when historians devote themselves to an evaluation of the conditions that permitted the escalation of the Vietnam war on May 1, 1970, will the full story be known.

At this moment (June 1970), with the decision to invade Cambodia, the United States is no longer conducting a separate "limited war" in Vietnam, an air war against North Vietnam, and a "special war" against Laos. The decision to invade Cambodia converted the involvements in Vietnam into a single aggressive war against *all the people of Indochina.*

President Norodom Sihanouk, in a recent interview, is quoted as saying: "Before the arrival of the French colonialists, Indochina did not exist. There was Vietnam, Laos and

Cambodia. It was the French that put it altogether inside a Federation." [7]

The effect of the Cambodian invasion of May 1, 1970, may well be the uniting of all liberation forces and resistance groups in all of the three Indochinese countries. But the Cambodian invasion also projects the underlying objectives of the United States in Asia as a whole. The Cambodian invasion brought about a qualitative change in the management of the war in Asia.

The Tet offensive of February and March of 1968 so dislodged the American military forces in Vietnam that open, unrestrained terror was let loose against the Vietnamese people by way of re-escalation. In considering the Song My massacre in Chapter Seven above, we briefly referred to the effect on American troops of that offensive. The effect of that offensive on American confidence in winning the war in Vietnam was revealed by a story in the *Wall Street Journal* of February 23, 1968, in which the writer suggests that the American people must get ready—if they aren't so yet—for the prospect that the whole U.S. effort in Vietnam may fail.

On March 11, 1968, in his editorial in *Newsweek,* Walter Lippmann stated that in his opinion the United States is certain to be beaten in Vietnam. When, in March 1968, President Johnson declared his unavailability for renomination for the presidency, the critical military situation in Vietnam may have compelled his decision. The deplorable state of the United States Army that was exposed during the Tet offensive brought about the retirement of General William C. Westmoreland and the replacement of Secretary of State Robert McNamara by Clark Clifford.

It was undoubtedly President Johnson's hope that a new administration might find avenues to peace denied to him during the four years he acted as Commander-in-Chief of the United States forces in Vietnam.

The actual state of demoralization of the American forces in Vietnam during the invasion was revealed by the role played by generals directly in command of the territory where the Song My massacres occurred. Major General Samuel W. Koster was charged with dereliction of duty during the massacre episodes. After the Army report investigating the Song My massacre was released, the following observations were made: "Whatever the degree of Koster's implication in the cover-up, many of the top brass felt considerable sympathy for him. 'You've got to see his predicament in the context of the time,' said one senior officer last week. '—the Tet offensive had just occurred, he had a brand-new outfit militarily slapped together, which was not his fault, and his troops were in a hard-core VC area where even a six-year-old boy can throw a grenade at you. I'd hate to be in his spot, and I'd hate to judge him.' "[8]

It was hoped that the Paris Peace Conference would promote negotiations that could bring peace to the people in that area.

During President Nixon's first year in office all the Vietnam antiwar groups in Congress and the university campuses toned down their activities to almost a whisper. The October–November 1969 Vietnam Moratorium forces almost disbanded. It was all in the hope that President Nixon, with a free hand, could bring peace.

The Cambodian invasion of May 1970 suggests that President Nixon is facing opposition to the continuation of the Vietnam war in his own official family. President Nixon has repeatedly asserted that the only alternative to his Vietnamization program is the "defeat and humiliation" of the United States. He has also announced his determination not to accept this "first defeat" in our nation's history.[9]

The forces that appear to have influenced the decision to invade Cambodia are the National Security Council; the Joint Chiefs of Staff; General Creighton Abrams, current Commander in Vietnam; and Henry Kissinger, the President's aide and adviser in matters of national security. The only explanation for the exclusion of Secretary of Defense Laird and Secretary of State Rogers from the conferences making the decision to invade Cambodia, a neutral country which in no way appeared to want an invasion, is that they were against further escalation.

President Nixon was by no means unaware of the dangers that were implicit in the invasion of Cambodia.

On March 14, 1970, General Matthew B. Ridgway (now retired), United Nations and United States Commander in Japan, Korea, and the Far East, and later Army Chief of Staff, contributed an article to the *Times* entitled "Settlement—Not Victory—in Vietnam." General Ridgway stated, in part:

> Many continue to argue that a military solution, or "victory," in Vietnam has all along been within our reach, that nothing less would serve our interests. I believe such a solution is not now and never has been possible *under conditions consistent with our interests*. . . .
>
> The basic decision, which I believe is irrevocable and which was made and announced long ago, was to reduce our operations and to initiate disengagement and withdrawal according to a plan merely outlined.
>
> Whether or not it includes an ancillary decision to complete withdrawal by a fixed date, I do not know, though I assume it does. For reasons of its own—and reasonable ones are not lacking—the Administration has not seen fit to announce it. . . .

> . . . *Certainly we should repudiate once and for all the search for a military solution and move resolutely along the path of disengagement and eventual complete withdrawal.* . . . [Emphasis added.]

United States aggression in Vietnam and the illegal invasion of Cambodia on May 1, 1970, can be fully understood only when examined in the perspective of history, especially history since the end of World War II.

Japan, defeated in 1945, was eclipsed as a military force in Asia.

France, between 1945 and 1954, attempted to retrieve her position in Asia but suffered a humiliating defeat at Dienbienphu in May 1954.

The Netherlands withdrew from Indonesia and accepted the change as final, without further military resistance.

The British too, in 1947, accepted changes in their status in India and elsewhere in Asia. The Commonwealth expects, by 1971, to be completely free of its commitments in Asia.

Regrettably, United States foreign policy since the end of World War II has refused to recognize the forces of change. Under that policy we have undertaken to assert political and economic power in the areas abandoned by Japan, France, the Netherlands, and Britain.

Walter Lippmann, interviewed by a writer for the London *Sunday Times* in October 1969, saw Americans as trying to throw off "a minor dark age." He is quoted as saying:

> The error is not merely the trouble in Vietnam, but the error lies in the illusion that the position occupied in the world by the United States at the end of the war was a permanent arrangement of power in the world. . . . This

> miscalculation has falsified all our other calculations—what our power was, what we could afford to do, what influence we had to exert in the world.

What have bcen some of our "miscalculations"? First and foremost, the policy which dominates almost all of our acts is the one enunciated in the Truman Doctrine of 1947. Under this doctrine the United States undertook as its responsibility the containment of communism by its willingness "to help free peoples to maintain their free institutions and their national integrity against aggressive movements that seek to impose on them totalitarian regimes." [10]

In 1947, while commenting on the rising tide of anti-Communist hysteria, Professor John K. Fairbank, one of America's most distinguished authorities on Chinese affairs, made the following significant observations:

> Our fear of Communism, partly as an expression of our general fear of the future, will continue to inspire us to aggressive anti-Communist policies in Asia and elsewhere, [and] the American people will be led to think and may honestly believe that the support of anti-Communist governments in Asia will somehow defend the American way of life. This line of American policy will lead to American aid to establish regimes which attempt to suppress the popular movements in Indonesia, Indochina, the Philippines, and China. . . . Thus, after setting out to fight Communism in Asia, the American people will be obliged in the end to fight the peoples of Asia.[11]

This book has recounted instances in which the United States took aggressive action with the purported authority of a world policeman—Guatemala in 1954; Lebanon in 1958; Cuba in 1962, etc.

In the Cuban situation the United States quarantine of that country brought us to the brink of nuclear war. (The full extent of United States intervention in Cuba is discussed in Appendix B.)

United States involvement in Asia commenced soon after October 1949, when Chiang Kai-Shek fled to Taiwan. In June 1950 the United States introduced a resolution before the United Nations Security Council to undertake resistance to the reported aggressive actions by the North Koreans.

Professor D. F. Fleming's monumental work, *The Cold War and Its Origins,* leaves some doubt whether the aggression actually was from North Korea to South Korea or from South Korea to North Korea.[12] The fact is that the United Nations police action in Korea began as a collective security action by members of the United Nations (the Soviet Union was boycotting the Security Council at the time, so no socialist veto was used). But as the war in Korea progressed the United Nations police action soon became an American operation, financed almost in its entirety by the United States and fought almost exclusively by United States armed forces.

In the 1951 election, Republican candidates Dwight D. Eisenhower and Richard M. Nixon promised the American people that American soldiers would be brought home from Korea soon afterward. By 1953 the Korean war was almost lost, and only measures that brought us perilously close to nuclear war made it possible to bring that sad episode to an end.

How near to nuclear war the United States came in Korea was revealed many years later. When Mr. Nixon was seeking the Republican nomination at Miami in August 1968, he was quoted as saying:

> How do you bring a war to a conclusion? I'll tell you how Korea was ended. . . . Eisenhower let the word go out—let the word go out diplomatically—to the Chinese and the North [Koreans] that he would not tolerate this continual ground war of attrition. And within a matter of months they negotiated. . . .[13]

Clearly a threat of the use of the atomic weapon is indicated.

On September 8, 1968, when he had become the candidate, Nixon referred to President Eisenhower's message during the Korean negotiations in the following terms: ". . . that unless they negotiated a complete truce in Korea, that the military consequences would be ones that would be unacceptable to them."[14]

Questioned about this remark, he denied the intention to use nuclear weapons in Korea, but there can be no doubt that the use of such weapons was not remote from his thinking.

Between January 28 and February 18, 1966, when the Senate Committee on Foreign Relations held its hearings on appropriations before Congress, the issue of U.S. involvement in Vietnam was again thoroughly aired. Senator Gore referred to the commitment of combat troops in Vietnam as being "one of the largest mistakes that we made." He went on:

> President Eisenhower said, "If there must be a war in Asia let it be Asians against Asians." President Kennedy said: "In the final analysis it is their war. They are the ones who have to win it or lose it. We can help them, we can give them equipment, we can send our men out there as advisers, but they have to win it, the people of Vietnam." And I recall when Vice President Johnson went to Vietnam in 1961, and he returned, and briefed this committee, and

> he was asked specifically if he had made a commitment to send American troops to Vietnam, his answer was "No." [15]

When President Johnson issued the orders to bomb Hanoi, in February 1965, the justification for our action was, presumably, to resist "aggression from the North," because United States security was at stake.

In Chapters Four and Five we discussed how the United States became involved in Vietnam and why our acts were illegal as well as acts of aggression. It seems clear that the order to bomb Hanoi was, in the main, motivated by the desire to fulfill American policy in Asia. And what was that policy?

Secretary of State Dean Rusk, in his appearance before the Senate Foreign Relations Committee on February 18, 1966, said in his prepared statement:

> Why are we in Vietnam? . . . we are in Vietnam because the issues posed there are deeply intertwined with our own security and because the outcome of the struggle can profoundly affect the nature of the world in which we and our children will live. The situation we face in Southeast Asia is obviously complex but, in my view, the underlying issues are relatively simple and are utterly fundamental. . . . We must recognize that what we are seeking to achieve in South Vietnam is part of a process that has continued for a long time—a process of preventing the expansion and extension of Communist domination by the use of force against the weaker nations on the perimeter of Communist power.[16]

During the Senate Foreign Relations Committee hearings at which Secretary of State Rusk testified, General Gavin stated that the Vietnam war should be terminated by a retreat to enclaves, and also that South Vietnam should be free to choose the type of government its people want.

Soon after the Committee hearings ended, Emmett John Hughes, former Special Assistant to President Eisenhower and an eminent political scientist, after a visit to Vietnam, detailed his views of conditions in that country, concluding his report as follows:

> . . . And it means the wisdom to sense that American repute in Asia is not dignified but diminished by untiring war for the unattainable victory . . . and American honor is not tarnished but brightened when so great a power can say, with quiet assurance: we have judged poorly, fought splendidly, and survive confidently.[17]

In November 1966 total United States deaths in action were 4,905. The "unattainable victory" that Emmett John Hughes referred to in May 1966 is still unattainable in 1970. The number of American casualties in battle has mounted to a total of 45,000 killed and 280,000 wounded, and we are no closer to victory today.

President Johnson wanted to terminate the Vietnam war "with victory." President Nixon wants to end the war "with honor." The acts of aggression which the United States has committed in Vietnam make it impossible to end the war "with honor." If our policy of containment of communism is not abandoned, it must follow logically that if in Korea, Thailand, Laos, or even Indonesia resistance to present governments commences and there is the threat of a communist take-over, then the United States will intervene.

Newsweek reported on October 27, 1969, that President Nixon made a private prediction to the directors of the Associated Press. "I will say confidently," the President declared, "that looking ahead just three years, the war will be over."

A few days before, Secretary of Defense Melvin R. Laird had stated at a Pentagon press conference: "Defense planning proceeds on the basis of providing forces for a big war in Europe and the support of two smaller ones in Asia. This includes a residual force for Vietnam.[18] Even if the Vietnam war is ended by negotiations, a "residual force" is expected to remain in Vietnam. The United States experience in Korea, where a residual force of 55,000 has been maintained since 1954, is that the war in that country is still not at an end. A residual force in Vietnam will mean that no matter what the basis for terminating the Vietnam war may be, the war itself will not actually be at an end.

The Vietnamese, North and South, know that the presence of United States forces means an unending war, and they are not likely to settle on those terms.

On October 15, 1969, Vietnam Moratorium Day was observed by an outpouring of people from all sections of the country and from all sections of life. According to *Life* magazine of October 24, 1969, the expression of public dissent was unrestrained and impressive.

Life magazine reporters who interviewed men in the field of war near Saigon concluded that "many soldiers regard organized anti-war campaigns in the United States with open and outspoken sympathy."

If in October 1969 the *Life* magazine reporter found that "many soldiers" were sympathetic to the antiwar campaign in the United States, we can assume that that sympathy has by no means diminished, but actually increased since then.

The *New York Times* of June 21, 1970, carried a front page story captioned "Indochina War Is Stirring Dissension on a Widening Scale Within the Ranks of the Army."[19] This *Times* report was made after a two-week tour of four Army bases in North Carolina, South Carolina, Alabama, and Kansas. The salient observations are that ". . . there was a recurring undercurrent of questioning, of hostility toward the military in general as well as to the war, that seemed to go beyond the usual G.I. gripes and to parallel the disaffection in what servicemen call the 'real world.' . . . Citizen soldiers . . . tend to take their attitude toward the war into the service with them. . . ."

"The continuing demand for manpower to sustain operations in Indochina has drawn into the armed services—particularly the Army with its heavy dependence on the draft—a broad cross section of an American public that is deeply divided over the war."

Into the *Congressional Record* was inserted a letter written by a Marine officer to his father, Senator William B. Saxbe, Republican Senator from Ohio. The letter, in part, reads as follows:

> I'm going to have to risk my life in Southeast Asia within the next year; risking my life in a war that hasn't been declared, can't be fought and can't be won; a war that is contrary to everything I've been taught to believe about America. . . . For the last decade, Americans have been electing men who said they had the solutions. . . . President Nixon pledged to put an end to the insanity and the war, fight inflation, promote continued social reform and bring us together. Promises have been compromised, the war has been expanded as it was in 1964 and 1968, the economy has gone to hell, racism has been ignored and the Government has made a strong effort to polarize the country into two hostile camps with no middle ground. . . .

Commenting on his son's letter, Senator Saxbe observed: "Violence breeds violence and once unleashed cannot be recaptured or controlled." [20]

But the American public that is opposed to the war is not restricted to the "articulate dissidents." C. Wright Mills' "power elite" seems to have had enough. The multinational corporations, the foundation technocrats, the international bankers, and the major news media all underestimated the resistance of the Vietnamese people.

After more than five years of war against a small nation the "power elite" has determined to bring the war to an end. Opposed to the wishes of the power elite, of course, is ranged the military-industrial complex. This "odd twin" stands to profit from most of $30 billion which was added to the country's military budget. (Could it be that President Nixon's decision to invade Cambodia was in the main influenced by the military-industrial complex to the exclusion of the rest of his Cabinet and government advisers?)

On April 15, 1970, Louis B. Lundborg, Chairman of the Board of the Bank of America, testified before the Senate Committee on Foreign Relations. Mr. Lundborg told the Committee, in part:

> In my judgment, the war in Vietnam is a tragic national mistake.
>
> I see no profit to the country in trying to fix the blame for what is past. . . .
>
> In my judgment, it is time the shareholders of America—the people—begin to call for an end to the squandering of American blood, morale and resources on what is in essence an Asian war of nationalism. . . .
>
> The revulsion against our posture in Vietnam has been so strong that it has colored and distorted the attitude of our people, and particularly of our young people, toward military service of any kind. . . .
>
> The overriding question is this one—"Does the United States from either a practical or moral viewpoint have either the right or the might to set itself up as the unilateral

> policeman for the world?" My answer to that question is that such a position is morally indefensible and practically unsustainable.*

College commencements of June 1970 found the campuses in a virtual turmoil. Strike actions of one sort or another were reported at more than 400 colleges and universities—including most of the biggest and most prestigious—and at countless high schools and secondary schools. It seems that the explosion that was touched off by the Cambodian invasion was evidence of a situation qualitatively different from those which followed the situation in the spring of 1968, when students declared that they would prefer "prison to service" (see Chapter Two.)

Business Week, in its May 16, 1970, editorial, assessed the situation as follows:

> If the events of the past two weeks have done nothing else, they should have convinced the U.S. that the student protest movement has to be taken seriously. Until now, it probably has been fair to say that the student activists were a minority. This no longer is true. The invasion of Cambodia and the senseless shooting of four students at Kent State University in Ohio have consolidated the academic community against the war, against business, and against government. . . .
>
> What brought the situation to a head was the enlargement of the war and the shooting at Kent State. At that point, the previously hesitant majority swung over to join the long-time dissenters. What had been a small, though vociferous, movement suddenly became a cause.

---

* Copies of Mr. Lundborg's address may be obtained from "Business Executives Move for Vietnam Peace and New National Priorities," 901 N. Howard Street, Baltimore, Maryland 21201.

Newsweek of June 15, 1970, carried a feature story entitled "Universities in Ferment." The writer observed that "in sheer scope, disruption of normal activity this year far outstrips anything that had gone before." At Columbia University 1,000 graduates, students, and sympathizers denounced the Indochina war by walking out on President Andrew W. Cordier's commencement speech to stage their own "counter-commencement." Comparable actions took place at Vassar College, University of California at Berkeley, Boston University, Oberlin College, Tufts University, and others.

Newsweek's editors concluded that a deep pessimism pervades the campuses today, that the days ahead seem bleak. Julian H. Levi, professor of urban studies at the University of Chicago, observes that the outlook is indeed bleak. "The Universities are in greater trouble than they have been for generations. I have serious doubts whether they can survive." [21]

President Nixon's Cambodian venture also deeply disturbed McGeorge Bundy, who served as adviser to Presidents Johnson and John F. Kennedy and is now president of the Ford Foundation. In a speech delivered at the University of Texas on May 15, 1970, Mr. Bundy referred to his role in the making of the 1965 decision to invade Vietnam, stating, "I have no desire to duck that responsibility." But Mr. Bundy declared: "Not only must there be no new incursions of Americans across the Cambodian border, but nothing that feels like that to the American people must happen again on the President's say-so alone. . . . The point is, quite simply, that any major action of this general sort, if undertaken in the same fashion as the Cambodian decision—now that the domestic effects of that decision are visible—would tear the country and the administration to pieces. At the very least the Congress would stop money for the war, and the chances of general domestic upheaval would be real."[22]

11:

A Dunkirk, a Dienbienphu, or a Hiroshima

Notwithstanding President Nixon's report to the nation on June 3, 1970, stating that "We have captured more than 10 million rounds of ammunition . . . 15,000 rifles, 2,000 mortars . . . 11 million pounds of rice," the Cambodian invasion of May 1, 1970, will be characterized by military historians as a fiasco and a colossal blunder. Traditionally military success is measured by the ground gained, military forces captured, and enemy forces dislodged. The commanding general in the field, the Joint Chiefs of Staff and the National Security Council, all of whom together appear to have made the decision to invade, were either ignorant of the character of the Cambodian "sanctuaries" or were misinformed by the C.I.A. and their own intelligence forces. The 30,000 troops, when they came upon the Cambodian "sanctuaries," found that not a single North Vietnamese or Vietcong soldier had been captured and that the ammunition (cashe counts) captured was negligible since it could be easily replaced.

On May 4, 1970, Premier Kosygin called a special conference and indicated emphatically that the Soviet Union would not falter in its assistance to the Vietnamese people. Mao Tse-tung made similar commitments.[1]

All President Nixon could boast of on June 3, 1970, was that "Seizing these weapons and ammunition will save American lives. Because of this operation, American soldiers who might not otherwise be ever coming home will now be coming home." A Pyrrhic victory; a sad commentary.

What President Nixon did not report to the people—and perhaps he failed to do so because his intelligence officers had not told him—is that while the "sanctuaries" along the Cambodian border are being destroyed, all the rest of Cambodia is being turned into a solid block of enemy territory.

For more than five years the United States has committed to Vietnam more than 500,000 field troops plus almost unlimited naval and air support. Aiding us were purported "allies" who are today (June 1970) being exposed as nothing more nor less than "mercenaries."

American schoolchildren's history books have customarily attacked the government of King George III because he hired German mercenaries to fight for Great Britain in the American Revolution. In Vietnam all of our "allies," with the exception of Australia and New Zealand (whose contributions are token), are "mercenaries." The Philippine army engineers who were sent to Vietnam were sent at a price of $38 million.[2]

Under a secret agreement entered into in 1967 the United States has been paying Thailand $50 million a year for sending a combat division to South Vietnam. To encourage Thailand to assign this 11,000-man unit the United States also agreed to increase its military assistance by $30 million for two years and to supply Thailand with a battery of Hawk anti-aircraft missiles.[3]

What secret agreements exist between the United States and Korea indicating the exact cost of the mercenaries from that country has not as yet been revealed. But reports are extant that financial arrangements exist between the United States Government and Korea which call for the payment of Korean forces assigned to Vietnam. And what other "secret" agreements has the United States made or does it plan to make throughout the world?

On June 13, 1970, the *Times* carried a dispatch from Washington which was captioned "Indochina Debate in Senate Shifts to Mercenary Issues." Legislation was under consideration to prohibit the President from entering into any agreement "to provide military instruction in Cambodia or to provide persons to engage in any combat activity in support of Cambodian forces." Some of the debate was as follows:

> Sen. Murphy: I do not consider these people mercenaries. They are not being hired by the United States to fight for the United States. They are asking for arms from the U.S. with which to defend their own freedom, their own right to self-determination, and their own right to carry out the policies of this Nation fixed by the last four Presidents. (Sic!)
>
> Sen. Aiken: Is the Senator aware that it is far more profitable for the soldiers of some governments to fight in Vietnam than to fight insurgents in their own country? That a Thai lieutenant general receives $370 if he stays at home? He receives a $450 bonus if he goes to Vietnam. That makes a total of $820 in all. And that applies all down the line. Is the Senator aware that a captain in Thailand receives $70 a month at home and that we pay him a $150 bonus, making $220 if he goes to Vietnam? So, when we talk about their not being mercenaries, I think the fact that they can get twice as much by fighting for us in a

> foreign country as they can by protecting their own country answers the question.[4]

Since President Nixon has committed himself to withdraw all American forces from Cambodia by June 30, 1970, the Senate is clearly concerned that Cambodia will be turned into a new Vietnam. During the Senate debate, Senator John J. Williams, Republican of Delaware, expressed deep concern about Congress's responsibility for regulating arms sales. He declared:

> First we sell arms to a country, then we send advisers to show them how to use these arms, then we send troops to protect the advisers. And that's how America gets into wars these days.[5]

The Cambodian invasion has not only turned that country into a new theater of war but actually constitutes a new chapter in the fulfillment of the Containment Policy of 1947. The United States today maintains more than 250 bases located in thirty countries, and the move into Cambodia constitutes the establishment of another base to be used in the struggle for the ultimate encirclement of China.

The Cambodian invasion brings into focus the situation to which Professor John K. Fairbank adverted, when in 1947 he perceptively observed that

> This line of American policy will lead to American aid to establish regimes which attempt to suppress the popular movements in Indonesia, Indochina, the Philippines and China. . . . Thus after setting out to fight communism in Asia, the American people will be obliged in the end to fight the peoples of Asia.[6]

The Cambodian invasion has still another effect. Not only has Cambodia become a solid block where all liberation forces can unite, but the whole Indochina peninsula is being alarmed by the invasion of a "neutral country." If the former states of French Indochina could be occupied by a Western power in 1970, what could be the effect of this invasion of the states in the vast geopolitical Indochina which stretches from the borders of East Pakistan to the Pacific Ocean and which includes Burma, Malaya, Thailand, Cambodia, Laos, Vietnam, and Indonesia? Are they all to be turned into client states to supply mercenaries for the ultimate showdown with China? (A careful reading of the Report of the United States Senate Hearings, entitled "The Truth about Vietnam," January 28 to February 18, 1966, indicates the ultimate U.S. goal in Asia. These hearings had as witnesses the following administration spokesmen: Secretary of State Dean Rusk; Lieutenant General James M. Gavin, retired; the Honorable George F. Kennan; General Maxwell D. Taylor; and the Honorable David D. Bell, Administrator, Agency for International Development.)

The departure of all United States forces from Cambodia on June 30, 1970, will not bring the invasion of that neutral country to an end. President Nguyen Van Thieu of South Vietnam as of June 13, 1970, predicted that his forces would be engaged in a long war in Cambodia and that American troops would remain in his country for "several years more." Mr. Thieu estimated that it would take four or five years for his government to stabilize its economic and military situation. Meanwhile, he said, the United States must support the South Vietnam war effort in Cambodia and take primary responsibility for blocking the Ho Chi Minh trail into Laos.[7]

Whether President Thieu's statement is supported by another secret agreement or not is really not relevant. President Nixon, at best, does not expect to withdraw more than 150,000 men by the spring of 1971. Whether that commitment will be kept now that South Vietnamese forces are replacing U.S. forces being withdrawn from Cambodia raises another question. But President Thieu also stated that he expects to be occupied in Cambodia another four or five years and that he will rely on U.S. support while he is so occupied. Presumably Mr. Thieu expects that U.S. troops will remain in Vietnam at least during these four or five years.

The "power elite," the American youth, and the American people will not allow two third-rate diplomats like President Nguyen Van Thieu and Vice-President Nguyen Cao Ky to determine how much more blood and American resources will be squandered in Asia.

If President Nixon does not agree to a policy of complete withdrawal from Asia, the United States may suffer a humiliating defeat in many ways more disastrous than the defeat suffered by the French at Dienbienphu in 1954.

President Nixon may, of course, resort to the reckless alternative of the employment of atomic weapons—tactical or otherwise.

We have already adverted to the observation made by President Nixon when he was a candidate for the presidency in 1968. At the time of the battle of Dienbienphu in the spring of 1954, Admiral Radford and Secretary John Foster Dulles proposed to the French generals and political leaders that atomic bombs be used to relieve the garrison at Dienbienphu. The plan was known as Operation Vulture. What Vice-President Nixon's views were at that time is not too clear. But on March 17, 1955, Nixon told the Executive Club of Chicago the following:

> . . . Our artillery and our tactical air force in the Pacific are now equipped with atomic explosives which can and will be used on military targets with precision and effectiveness.
>
> . . . It is foolish to talk about the possibility that the weapons which might be used in the event war breaks out in the Pacific would be limited to the conventional Korean and World War II types of explosives. Our forces could not fight an effective war in the Pacific with those types of explosives if they wanted to. Tactical atomic explosives are now conventional and will be used against the military targets of any aggressive force.[8]

In light of the above statement of March 17, 1955 in Chicago, President Nixon's lack of memory that he had intended to use atomic weapons in Korea, when he was questioned about it in the summer of 1968, most blatantly puts in doubt President Nixon's veracity.

What tactical-atomic weapons are is not too clear. But that the mention of them can be treated as a threat is borne out by the broad allusions made by President Nixon at his May 8, 1970, press conference when he observed that the Cambodian involvement was a purposeful move to eliminate sanctuaries and that if there is a major enemy action it would meet consequences.

President Nixon places much reliance on his Vietnamization program. If that program envisages a gradual and continuous reduction of American troops and replacement by Vietnamese troops, then it does not require the erudition of a Clausewitz to understand that the Saigon Army must capitulate soon after our combat troops are removed.

If, for instance, the N.L.F. and the Vietcong decide to reduce their activities during the period when the U.S. combat forces are being withdrawn, this cannot be accepted as an abandonment by the N.L.F. and Vietcong of their opposition to the Saigon regime as constituted at present. What must be assumed is that while the United States combat forces are being withdrawn, the N.L.F. and Vietcong will be free to prepare for another Tet offensive which will undoubtedly decimate the Saigon forces fighting only with our *support* troops. In such an eventuality the Nixon administration will be faced with one of three choices: a re-escalation of our forces, a Dunkirk, or a Hiroshima.

Since the American people, in light of the Cambodian adventure, will not accept a re-escalation, and since President Nixon will not countenance a Dunkirk, our ultimate choice must be a Hiroshima.

During a Senate debate in June 1970 on a bill to limit President Nixon's powers to recommit troops in Cambodia, an amendment was adopted by a substantial majority reserving to the President the right to use almost any force to protect the lives of American troops in the field.

Let us assume that by 1971 there remain only 200,000 troops in Vietnam or even less, and the civil war in Vietnam continues unabated, and President Nixon and his newly constituted coterie of advisers—the Joint Chiefs of Staff, the National Security Council, and Mr. Henry A. Kissinger—and the commander in the field declare that American troops are endangered. Then there is a possibility that tactical-nuclear weapons will be used.

That it is not only scaremongers who fear the possible use of nuclear weapons in Vietnam is attested by an interview in the *New York Times* of May 17, 1970, with Richard E. Neustadt, professor of government at Harvard and the U.S. political science profession's leading authority on the presidency. Professor Neustadt recalled that previous chiefs of staff had suggested using tactical nuclear weapons when problems arose in Asia. He asked: "Are we to be told at some future date that the safety of our troops, or the necessity for avoiding defeat, requires nuclear bombing of the Ho Chi Minh Trail or of Haiphong harbor?" The professor said, "I'm not suggesting that Nixon has any such intention, but his talk about no defeat and no humiliation makes that kind of scenario a nightmare for me." [9]

On May 20, 1970, Mr. Richard Barnet * addressed the "Business Executives Move for Vietnam Peace" on the subject of "Will the President Use Nuclear Weapons?" He adverted to the presence of nuclear weapons in the Southeast Asia area, including Korea and Thailand, and concluded his address with the following observation:

> There is no reason, if in fact we are not going to use those nuclear weapons, that they should be there. The threat that we are going to use them, or reserve the options to use them, can only have the effect of bringing this war into a much greater conflagration and convince the other side that we have absolutely no intention of negotiating or of getting out.[10]

Mr. Barnet addressed the Multi-National Lawyers Conference on Vietnam, Laos and Cambodia, at Toronto, Canada, on May 23, 1970. The title of his address was "Use of Nuclear Weapons in Indo-China," in which he observed that

---

* Mr. Richard Barnet is a recognized authority on problems of national security and arms control. He is a graduate of Harvard College and Harvard Law School. During the Kennedy administration, he served in the State Department and the United States Arms Control and Disarmament Agency and was later consultant at the Department of Defense. Mr. Barnet's most recent books are: *Intervention and Revolution* (1968) and *The Economics of Death* (1969).

> As of 1968 there were more than 5,500 nuclear weapons in the Southeast Asia area. Most of these weapons are aboard carriers and can be brought to Vietnam extremely rapidly. A substantial number of nuclear weapons are located on the mainland in Korea. Nuclear weapons are also located in Thailand, according to reliable reports of knowledgeable Pentagon officials and military officers.[11]

Alexander the Great, while organizing the Greek phalanxes in preparation for the wars against the Persians, advised the Greek generals that "ONE DOES NOT GATHER SPEARS TO SIT UPON THEM."

President Nixon too does not gather tactical nuclear weapons merely to sit upon them.

It would be tragic indeed if the use of the ultimate weapon depended upon the advice of that group that was responsible for the Cambodian invasion . . .

Einstein, like Isaiah, tried to tell us of the enormity of the disaster that we are facing when he said that the Fourth World War would be fought with rocks.

APPENDIX A:

U.S. Intervention in Vietnam Is Not Legal*

Satire and sarcasm often have been weapons of effective, if deluding, advocacy. The article by Eberhard P. Deutsch, "The Legality of the United States Position in Vietnam," in the May 1966 issue of the *American Bar Association Journal* (p. 436) is a classical demonstration of this technique. The author takes issue with the Lawyers Committee on American Policy Towards Vietnam, as expressed in its memorandum of law, on the following fundamental questions: (1) The right of self-defense under the United Nations Charter; (2) Violations of the Geneva Accords; (3) Sanctions by the SEATO Treaty; and (4) Violations of our own Constitution.

But the author concludes with the statement that the memorandum of the Lawyers Committee "is grounded on an emotional attitude opposed to United States policy, rather than on law." He seeks to demonstrate this by quoting the *concluding* paragraph of a twenty-six-page, carefully documented statement of the applicable law, which in pero-

* Reprinted from the *American Bar Association Journal,* July 1966.

ration states in the very last sentence: "Should we not spell the end of the system of unilateral action . . . that has been tried for centuries—and has always failed?"

The author then wields the weapon of sarcasm by contrasting the Lawyers Committee memorandum with the "temperate statement of thirty-one professors of law from leading law schools throughout the United States." The statement of these professors appears in the *Congressional Record* of January 27, 1966 (p. A410), and the entirety of that statement is:

> As teachers of international law we wish to affirm that the presence of U.S. forces in South Vietnam at the request of the Government of that country is lawful under general principles of international law and the United Nations Charter. The engagement of U.S. forces in hostilities at the request of the Government of South Vietnam is a legitimate use of force in defense of South Vietnam against aggression. We believe that the evidence indicates that the United States and South Vietnam are taking action that attacks neither the territorial integrity nor the political independence of the People's Republic of Vietnam—action that seeks only to terminate aggression originating in North Vietnam.

This one-paragraph "temperate statement" is not buttressed by a single citation or authority. What is particularly deplorable is that it was issued in November of 1965 as a rebuttal to the committee's memorandum, which was issued in late September 1965.

The author of the "legality position" article then contrasts the Lawyers Committee memorandum with "the simple resolution adopted unanimously on February 21, 1966, by the House of Delegates of the American Bar Association." This resolution, in a concluding one-sentence statement, asserts that "the position of the United States in Vietnam is legal under international law, and is in accordance with the Charter of the United Nations and the South-East Asia Treaty." The House of Delegates' resolution, too, does not support its conclusion with a single citation or authority.

When the *Harvard Law Record* on March 10 contrasted the memorandum of law of the Lawyers Committee with the "simple resolution" adopted by the House of Delegates, it had this to say: "Viewed against the background of the *sober and erudite* Lawyers Committee brief and Arthur Krock's research, the ABA resolution contributes little to the national dialogue on Vietnam." [Emphasis added.]

The satirical technique of the author of the "legality position" article is worthy of an undergraduate debater, but not of the respected Chairman of the American Bar Association Committee on Peace and Law Through United Nations. He does, indeed, wrestle earnestly with four basic propositions discussed by the Lawyers Committee, and it is to these propositions that I shall address myself.

I. Unilateral Intervention Violates the United Nations Charter

The writer of the "legality position" article discusses the first exception of Article 51 of the Charter of the United Nations, which reads: "Nothing in the present Charter shall impair the *inherent* right of individual or collective self-defense *if* an armed attack occurs against a Member of the United Nations, until the Security Council has taken the measures necessary to maintain international peace and security." [Emphasis added.]

He asserts that "A thesis that members of the United Nations are not permitted to participate in collective self-defense to repel aggression, on the ground that the aggrieved nation is not a member of the United Nations, can hardly be supported on its face, in reason, logic or law." He cites as authority two distinguished writers.[1]

The Lawyers Committee in its memorandum concludes that Article 51 does not permit the United States to act unilaterally in the "collective self-defense" of Vietnam because Article 51 applies only if an armed attack occurs against a member of the United Nations.

This limitation was not inadvertent. It was the result of careful draftsmanship by Senator Arthur H. Vandenberg, who "was the principal negotiator in the formulation of this text" of Article 51.[2] In a statement of June 13, 1945, before the United Nations Commission that drafted Article 51, Senator Vandenberg said: ". . . [W]e have here recognized the inherent right of self-defense, whether individual or collective, which permits any sovereign state among us [*i.e.*, members of the United Nations] or any qualified regional group of states to ward off attack. . . ."[3]

Secretary of State Edward R. Stettinius, Jr., noted the following on May 21, 1945: "The parties to any dispute . . . should obligate themselves first of all to seek a solution by negotiation, mediation, conciliation, arbitration or judicial settlement, *resort to regional agencies or arrange-*

---

[1] Bowett, Self-defense in International Law 193–195 (1958); Kelsen, The Law of the United Nations 793 (1950).

[2] The quoted words are from a memorandum, "Participation in the North Atlantic Treaty of States Not Members of the United Nations," dated April 13, 1949, prepared by the Office of the Legal Adviser, Department of State, and reproduced in 5 Whiteman, Digest of International Law 1068.

[3] Memorandum, *op. cit.* supra note 2, in 5 Whiteman, Digest of International Law 1068, 1072.

ment or other peaceful means of their own choice." [Emphasis in original.] [4]

Professor Julius Stone states: "The license [of individual and collective self-defense] does not apparently cover even an 'armed attack' against a *non-Member*." [Emphasis in original.] [5]

Furthermore, the United States has acknowledged that the right of "collective self-defense" applies to Vietnam only if it becomes a member of the United Nations. On September 9, 1957, in arguing before the Security Council for the admission of Vietnam to the United Nations, Henry Cabot Lodge, our representative, stated: "The people of Vietnam . . . ask now only . . . to enjoy the benefits of collective security, the mutual help which membership in the . . . United Nations offers." [6]

This does not mean, of course, that a nonmember state or entity does not have the "inherent" right of self-defense or that nonmember states may be attacked with impunity. But it does mean that in case of an attack upon a nonmember state it is for the United Nations to decide upon the necessary measures to be taken by its member states and not for any state to decide for itself that it will employ arms for "collective self-defense."

During the Suez crisis President Eisenhower said: "The United Nations is *alone* charged with the responsibility of securing the peace in the Middle East and throughout the world." [Emphasis added.] [7]

---

[4] 12 Dep't. State Bull. 949–950 (1945).

[5] STONE, LEGAL CONTROLS OF INTERNATIONAL CONFLICT 244 (1954).

[6] U.N. SECURITY COUNCIL OFF. REC., 790th meeting 5.

[7] 4 UNITED NATIONS ACTION IN THE SUEZ CRISIS: INTERNATIONAL LAW IN THE MIDDLE EAST CRISIS—(Tulane Studies in Political Science, Vol. IV (1956).

And at the same time, Secretary of State John Foster Dulles characterized as "unthinkable" a proposal that the United States and the Soviet Union act jointly to restore the peace in that area, saying that that was the function of the United Nations. He said:

> Any intervention by the United States and/or Russia or any other action, except by a duly constituted United Nations peace force, would be counter to everything the General Assembly and the Secretary-General of the United Nations were charged by the Charter to do in order to secure a United Nations police cease fire.[8]

The author of the "legality position" article confuses the right of an attacked nonmember state to defend itself with the lack of right of a member state to participate in that defense in the absence of United Nations authorization.

The issue is the lawfulness of the actions of the United States, which is both a nonattacked state and a member of the United Nations. It does not follow that because Vietnam has an "inherent" right to defend itself, the United States has an "inherent" right to decide for itself to participate unilaterally in that defense. Professor Hans Kelsen, one of the principal authorities relied upon by Mr. Deutsch, has pointed out this critical distinction: "It is hardly possible to consider the right or the duty of a non-attacked state to assist an attacked state as an 'inherent' right, that is to say, a right established by natural law." [9]

The argument also makes the United States its own judge to determine the occurrence of an "armed attack" in Vietnam, whereas Article 39 of the United Nations Charter

---

[8] New York Times, November 6, 1956.
[9] KELSEN, *op. cit.* supra note 1, at 797.

provides that "The Security Council shall determine the existence of any threat to the peace, breach of the peace, or act of aggression. . . ." But as Philip C. Jessup, now a Judge of the International Court of Justice, has noted:

> It would be *disastrous* to agree that every State may decide for itself which of the two contestants is in the right and may govern its conduct according to its own decision. . . . The ensuing conflict would be destructive to the ordered world community which the Charter and any modern law of nations must seek to preserve. State C would be shipping . . . war supplies to A, while State A would be assisting State B . . . and it would not be long before C and D would be enmeshed in the struggle out of "self-defense." [Emphasis added.] [10]

Acceptance of Mr. Deutsch's argument would destroy the concept of collective peacekeeping, which the Charter embodies, in the case of nonmember states or areas.

No Armed Attack Within Meaning of the Charter

The author of the "legality position" article also seeks to justify the United States intervention in Vietnam on the ground that "these attacks [against United States naval vessels] are part of a deliberate and systematic campaign of aggression," to quote the Congressional Joint Southeast Asia resolution of August 1964. The Lawyers Committee on American Policy Towards Vietnam takes the position that the occurrence of an armed attack within the meaning of the United Nations Charter has not been established.

Under the clear text of Article 51 of the Charter, the

---

[10] Jessup, A Modern Law of Nations 205 (1948).

right of self-defense arises only if an "armed attack" has occurred. The phrase "armed attack" has an established meaning in the Charter and in international law. It was deliberately employed because it does not easily lend itself to expedient elasticity or to arbitrary ambiguity.

"Self-defense" is not justified by every aggression or hostile act, but only in the case of an "armed attack," when the necessity for action is "instant, overwhelming, and leaving no moment for deliberation." This definition was classically stated by Secretary of State Daniel Webster in *The Caroline*[11] and affirmed in the Nuremberg judgment. It was codified in the Charter by unanimous vote of the General Assembly at its first session.[12]

This strict limitation of permissible self-defense to cases of an "armed attack" was at the time of the framing of the Charter being pressed by the United States, the Soviet Union, and Great Britain in the Nuremberg trials. The defense was offered that Germany was compelled to attack Norway to forestall an Allied invasion. In reply, the tribunal said: "It must be remembered that preventive action in foreign territory is justified only in case of 'an instant and overwhelming necessity for defense, leaving no choice of means, and no moment for deliberation.'" (The Caroline Case, Moore's Digest of International Law, II 412.)[13]

Thus, while any hostile act may be an aggression, not every aggression is an "armed attack," and forceful self-defense is not a permissible response unless there is an "armed attack."

On March 4, 1966, the Department of State issued "The

---

[11] 7 MOORE, DIGEST OF INTERNATIONAL LAW 919 (1906).

[12] U.N. GEN. ASS. OFF. REC. 1st Sess., RES. 95(I).

[13] INTERNATIONAL MILITARY TRIBUNAL (NUREMBERG) 171 (1946); BIN CHANG, GENERAL PRINCIPLES OF LAW 84 (1953).

Legality of United States Participation in the Defense of Vietnam." This fifty-two-page memorandum acknowledges that an "armed attack" is an essential condition precedent to the use of force in self-defense and that aggression is not enough. Astonishingly, however, it glosses over the crucial distinction between the two. While it alleges the occurrence of an armed attack "before February 1965," it fails to furnish any facts or details concerning such an attack. Indeed, it admits that it is unable to do so. This is not like the situation in Korea, where the Security Council found that an actual, visible, forcible invasion beyond the demarcation line had occurred at a specific time and place by large forces. This memorandum states that because of the "guerilla war in Viet Nam" (i.e., the indigenous character of the conflict) the State Department is unable to indicate when or where the "armed attack" began. It also admits that "the critical military element of the insurgency . . . is unacknowledged by North Viet Nam." The memorandum contends that acts of externally supported subversion, the clandestine supply of arms and the infiltration of armed personnel over the "years" preceding the direct intervention of the United States, "clearly constitutes an 'armed attack' under any reasonable definition."

These allegations, even if true (as appears below), indicate acts of aggression, but they do not show the occurrence of an armed attack "leaving no choice of means, and no moment for deliberation." [14]

Such acts were well known as forms of aggression when

[14] See the report of Senators Mike Mansfield, Edmund S. Muskie, Daniel K. Inouye, George D. Aiken and L. Caleb Boggs to the Senate Committee on Foreign Relations, dated January 6, 1966, entitled "The Vietnam Conflict: The Substance and the Shadow," hereafter referred to as the Mansfield report. It is reprinted in 112 CONG. REC. 140 (1966).

the Charter was drawn and long before. Nevertheless, the framers of the Charter rejected them as inadequate to justify the unilateral use of force. Except in the limited instance of an armed attack "leaving no choice of means, and no moment for deliberation," they left nations to the peace-keeping procedures of the United Nations for collective redress against aggression.

Furthermore, the State Department memorandum refutes its own charge of the occurrence of an "armed attack." The long-smoldering conditions of unrest, subversion, and infiltration cited in the memorandum are not acts that gave rise to such a need for an immediate response that "no choice of means, and no moment for deliberation" remained.

The memorandum does not sustain its charge of external aggression. It indicates that prior to 1964 the "infiltrators" from the North were South Vietnamese who were returning to the South. The lumping of "40,000 armed and unarmed guerillas" is not meaningful. Unarmed Vietnamese have an inherent right to move about in their own country. In the absence of the functioning of the International Control Commission, the subsequent movement of Vietnamese from one zone in Vietnam to another zone in Vietnam would appear to be an internal matter, not a violation of international law.

The Mansfield report (cited in footnote 14) shows that prior to 1965 infiltration of men from North Vietnam had been going on "for many years," but that this "was confined primarily to political cadres and military leadership until about the end of 1964." On the other hand, it notes, "In 1962, U.S. military advisers and service forces in South Vietnam totaled approximately 10,000 men." The Mansfield report makes plain that significant armed personnel were introduced from the North only after the United States had intervened to avoid the "total collapse of the Saigon government's authority [which] appeared imminent in the early months of 1965." The report states:

> U.S. combat troops in strength arrived at that point in response to the appeal of the Saigon authorities. The Vietcong *counter response* was to increase their military activity with forces strengthened by intensified *local* recruitment and infiltration of regular North Vietnamese troops. With the change in the composition of the opposing forces the character of the war also changed sharply. [Emphasis added.] [15]

The introduction of North Vietnamese forces as a counter response is also emphasized by the observation in the Mansfield report that by May 1965 about 34,000 United States service forces were in Vietnam and that "Beginning in June [1965] an estimated 1,500 North Vietnamese troops per month have entered South Vietnam. . . ." Significant forces from the North thus followed and did not precede the direct involvement of the United States.

Intervention Not Justified by "Collective Self-Defense"

The State Department memorandum is structured on the wholly untenable assumption that the conflict in South Vietnam is the result of external aggression ("an armed attack from the North") and is not a civil war. For if it is a civil war, the intervention of the United States is a violation of its solemn undertaking not to interfere in the internal affairs of other countries.

It is hardly open to dispute that the present conflict in

---

[15] Mansfield report, 112 Cong. Rec. 140, 141 (1966).

South Vietnam is essentially a civil war among what James Reston has described as a "tangle of competing individuals, regions, religions and sects . . . [among] a people who have been torn apart by war and dominated and exploited by Saigon for generations." [16]

The State Department memorandum itself shows that before 1964 the so-called infiltration was of South Vietnamese returning to their homeland. Even if they were returning for the purpose of participating in the fighting in South Vietnam, that still constitutes civil war by any definition.

The Declaration of Honolulu also implicitly concedes that the conflict had its origin in the internal situation in Vietnam and not in an external armed attack. The stress which the declaration places on the urgent need for basic social reform is an acknowledgment that the war is essentially a revolt against domestic conditions. To this may be added the existence of a desperate desire for peace and independence from foreign intervention, which all neutral reporters have observed.

The author of the "legality position" article also argues that the conflict arises from an external aggression. This is contradicted by his failure to consider the role played by the National Liberation Front; yet it does exist and is unquestionably in actual control of most of South Vietnam and the government in those areas. The only conceivable justification for the refusal of the United States to acknowledge the existence or the belligerent status of the National Liberation Front is that the front consists of rebels or insurgents. If that be so, then they are fighting their own government in a civil strife and are not foreign aggressors.

As stated by Benjamin V. Cohen in the Niles memorial

---

[16] New York Times, April 3, 1966.

lecture, "The United Nations in Its 20th Year": "True, the charter does not forbid civil war or deny the right to revolt. But it does not sanction the right of an outside state to participate in aother state's civil war." [17]

It cannot be asserted that South Vietnam is a separate "country" so far as North Vietnam is concerned. The Geneva Accords recognized Vietnam as but one country, of which South Vietnam is only an organic part. The Accords declared that the temporary military line that established the north and south military zones at the Seventeenth Parallel pending the elections "should not in any way be interpreted as a political or territorial boundary." (Section 6.) And Section 7 stated that the political settlement should be effected on the basis of "the independence, unity, and territorial integrity" of Vietnam.

But even if North Vietnam and South Vietnam are deemed separate entities in international law, the United States may not respond to the intervention of North Vietnam in the civil war in the South by bombing the North. There is no legal basis for responding to an intervention of one state in a civil war by a military attack on the territory of the intervening state. It is sobering to reflect that not even Germany under Hitler or Italy under Mussolini claimed that their intervention in behalf of Franco during the Spanish Civil War would have vindicated their use of military force upon the territory of another state intervening in behalf of the loyalists. And no country intervening in behalf of Spain's legitimate government asserted a right to respond by military force against Germany or Italy.

Therefore, even if North Vietnam were an intervening

---

[17] 111 CONG. REC. 2473 (1965). He cites COHEN, THE UNITED NATIONS, CONSTITUTIONAL DEVELOPMENTS, GROWTH AND POSSIBILITIES 53–54 (1961).

state so far as South Vietnam is concerned, under the legal position advanced by Mr. Deutsch, the bombing of the United States by North Vietnam would have as much legitimacy as does the bombing of North Vietnam by the United States.

II. U.S. Military Presence Violates Geneva Accords

The author of the "legality position" article suggests that United States intervention in Vietnam is not in violation of the Geneva Accords on the ground that "since their inception these accords have been violated continuously by Hanoi." He states that "It is an accepted principle of international law that a material breach of a treaty by one of the parties thereto dissolves the obligation of the other party, at least to the extent of withholding compliance until the defaulting party purges itself."

The Lawyers Committee takes the position that United States intervention is not justified by the purported breach of the Geneva Accords by Hanoi. The Accords embody two central principles: (1) recognition of the independence and freedom of Vietnam from foreign control and (2) the unification in the elections set in the Accords for 1956.

In its own pledge to observe the Geneva Accords, the United States recognized that the military participation in Vietnam was temporary and that, in any case, it was not political or geographic. Insofar as the United States referred to that country, it designated it as "Vietnam," not "South Vietnam" or "North Vietnam." The elections thus were to determine not whether North and South Vietnam should be united, but what the government of the single state of Vietnam should be. As the time for the arrangements for the elections approached, however, the Diem regime, which was then in control of South Vietnam, announced on July 16, 1955, that not only would it defy the provisions calling for national elections, but would not engage even in negotiations for modalities.

The reasons for not agreeing to the elections of 1956 are quite understandable. President Eisenhower told us that the actual reason the elections were not held was that "persons knowledgeable in Indo-Chinese affairs" believed that "possibly 80 per cent of the population would have voted for the Communist Ho Chi Minh." [18]

Under the Geneva Accords, the undertaking to hold the elections within two years was unconditional. The refusal of Saigon to hold the elections plainly violated one of the two central conditions that had made the Geneva Accords acceptable to all parties. That the Vietnam conflict ultimately did resume is, therefore, not surprising. For, as George McT. Kahin and John W. Lewis, professors of government at Cornell University, asked in a question wholly ignored by our State Department, "When the military struggle for power ends on the agreed condition that the competition will be transferred to the political level, can the side which violates the agreed conditions ultimately expect the military struggle will not be resumed?" [19]

The military involvement of the United States in Vietnam also violates the second essential provision of the Accords —the prohibition against the introduction of foreign troops and the establishment of military bases. Article 4 of the Geneva Accords prohibits the "introduction into Vietnam

---

[18] EISENHOWER, WHITE HOUSE YEARS: MANDATE FOR CHANGE, 1953–1956, 372 (1963).

[19] Bulletin of the Atomic Scientists, "The United States in Vietnam," June, 1965, page 28.

of foreign troops and military personnel," and Article 5 prohibits in Vietnam any "military base under the control of a foreign power." Therefore, it is the presence of 250,000 American troops and the installation in Vietnam of massive military bases under the control of the United States that violate these agreements, not the presence of North Vietnamese in Vietnam.

III. U.S. Intervention Violates SEATO Treaty

Mr. Deutsch also challenges the conclusion of the Lawyers Committee with respect to sanctions under the SEATO Treaty, which was adopted in September 1954. Article 1 of the Treaty provides:

> The parties undertake, as set forth in the United Nations Charter, to settle any international disputes in which they may be involved, by peaceful means . . . and to refrain in their international relations from the threat or use of force in any manner inconsistent with the purposes of the United Nations.

It must be pointed out that Article 53 of the United Nations Charter provides that "No enforcement action shall be taken under regional arrangements or by regional agencies, without the authority of the Security Council." Furthermore, Article 103 of the Charter provides:

> In the event of a conflict between the members of the United Nations under the present charter and their obligations under any other international agreement, their obligations under the present charter shall prevail.

The use of our ground forces since the spring of 1965 is sought to be justified under the provisions of the SEATO

Treaty. But extracts from the 1954 Senate debate on the Treaty demonstrate the fragility of this claim. In explaining the commitments under the SEATO Treaty to the Senate, Walter F. George, Chairman of the Senate Committee on Foreign Relations, made the following statements:

> The treaty does not call for automatic action; it calls for consolidation with other signatories. If any course of action shall be agreed . . . or decided upon, then that action must have the approval of Congress, because the constitutional process of each signatory government is provided for . . . it is clear that the threat to territorial integrity and political independence also encompasses acts of subversion . . . but even in that event the United States would not be bound to put it down. I cannot emphasize too strongly that we have no obligation . . . to take positive measures of any kind. All we are obligated to do is consult together about it.[20]

Richard N. Goodwin, a former Deputy Assistant Secretary of State, in a recent article discussing the significance of our reliance upon the SEATO agreement as the basis for our intervention in Vietnam, states, in part:

> One can search the many statements of Presidents and diplomats in vain for any mention of the SEATO Treaty. Time after time, President Johnson set forth the reasons for our presence in Vietnam, but he never spoke of the requirements of the treaty, nor did anyone at the State Department suggest that he should, even though they surely reviewed every draft statement. The treaty argument is, in truth, something a clever advocate conceived a few months ago.[21]

---

[20] 101 CONG. REC. 1051–1052 (1955).

[21] The New Yorker, "Reflections on Vietnam," April 16, 1966, page 57, and page 70.

Furthermore, the SEATO Treaty also clearly pledges the parties to respect the Geneva Declaration of 1954, which was agreed upon only a few months before the SEATO Treaty. The State Department memorandum of March 4, 1966, referred to above, significantly misquotes the SEATO Treaty on essential points. It asserts (Section IV B) that Article 4(1) of SEATO creates an "obligation to meet the common danger in the event of armed aggression." The term "armed aggression" is not to be found in the Treaty. Article 4(1) speaks of "aggression by means of armed attack." In case of such "armed attack," "each Party recognizes" that it "would endanger its own peace and safety, and agrees that it will in that event act to meet the common danger in accordance with its constitutional processes."

Hence, only in case of an "armed attack" (in the meaning of Article 51 of the United Nations Charter) would the United States have, at most, the right, but no obligation, to assist the "Free Territory of Vietnam" until it was to be unified by July 1956.

The invocation of the SEATO Treaty is the latest of the evershifting grounds which the State Department has advanced to sustain the lawfulness of its position. Arthur Schlesinger, Jr., has characterized this argument as an "intellectual disgrace." Arthur Krock has described its origin as follows:

> The President had utilized the provocation of the Tonkin Gulf attack on the Seventh Fleet by North Vietnamese gunboats to get a generalized expression of support from Congress. This worked well enough until it was argued, against the public record, as approval by Congress of any expansion of the war the President might make in an unforeseeable future. Then Rusk shifted the major basis for the claim to the SEATO compact.

But extracts from the 1954 Senate debate on the treaty demonstrate the fragility of this claim.[22]

The credibility of the argument that the SEATO Treaty furnished a legal justification for the President's action is also refuted by the fact that the State Department in its March 1965 memorandum, entitled "Legal Basis for United States Actions Against North Vietnam," did not even mention SEATO. Significantly, too, President Johnson in a press conference statement on July 28, 1965, explaining "why we are in Vietnam," made no mention of SEATO. This can hardly be squared with the present belated claim that the Treaty imposed an obligation upon the President to intervene in Vietnam.

Moreover, the invocation of SEATO does not advance the State Department's case. In the first place, Article 1 of the treaty is expressly subordinate to the provisions of the United Nations Charter, and Article 6 expressly acknowledges the supremacy of the Charter. Article 103 of the Charter, quoted above, subordinates all regional treaty compacts to the Charter, and Article 53 is explicit that "no enforcement action shall be taken under regional arrangements or by regional agencies without the authorization of the Security Council. . . ."

The United States is not obliged by SEATO to engage in any military undertaking in Vietnam even if it were otherwise permitted to do so under the Charter. As noted by Representative [now Secretary of Defense] Melvin R. Laird, the SEATO Treaty was "not a commitment to send American troops to fight in southeast Asia. It carefully avoided the

---

[22] The New York Times, "The Sudden Rediscovery of SEATO," March 6, 1966.

kind of automatic response to aggression embodied in the NATO agreement. . . ."[23]

Representative Laird pointed out that in soliciting the advice and consent of the Senate to the Treaty, Senator H. Alexander Smith of New Jersey, who was a member of the United States delegation to the Manila Conference at which the Treaty was negotiated and who was one of the signers of the Treaty for the United States, emphasized that "Nothing in this treaty calls for the use of American ground forces. . . ." On the floor of the Senate on February 1, 1955, he said:

> Some of the participants came to Manila with the intention of establishing . . . a compulsory arrangement for our military participation in case of any attack. Such an organization might have required the commitment of American ground forces to the Asian mainland. We carefully avoided any possible implication regarding an arrangement of that kind.
>
> We have no purpose of following any such policy as that of having our forces involved in a ground war. . . .
>
> For ourselves, the arrangement means that we will have avoided the impracticable overcommitment which would have been involved if we attempted to place American ground forces around the perimeter of the area of potential Chinese ingress into southeast Asia. Nothing in this treaty calls for the use of American ground forces in that fashion.[24]

Article 4, Section 2, is explicit that if South Vietnam were threatened "in any way other than by armed attack, the [SEATO] Parties shall consult immediately in order to

---

[23] 112 Cong. Rec. 5558 (1966).

[24] 101 Cong. Rec. 1052–1054 (1955).

agree on the measures which should be taken for the common defense."

SEATO therefore *prohibits* unilateral assistance action. Indeed, the Treaty originally required previous *agreement* among the other seven partners before any SEATO power could take any "measures," including nonmilitary measures, not to mention combat assistance. In 1964 the unanimity requirement was reinterpreted to mean that "measures" could be taken in the absence of a dissenting vote among the SEATO partners. The United States has not convened the SEATO powers because of the certainty of such a dissent. It can hardly claim, therefore, that SEATO *obligates* it to pursue its present course when in fact it is evading its Treaty obligation to obtain collective permission for "collective defense," as even the name of the Treaty indicates.

Finally, the United States actions also violate Article 53 of the United Nations Charter, quoted above, which unequivocally prohibits enforcement action under regional arrangements except with *previous* Security Council authorization. Hence, even if the United States had obtained the required consent from its SEATO partners, it would still need the authorization of the Security Council to make its "measures" legal.

Therefore, the United States, far from being obligated, is not permitted by SEATO or by the United Nations Charter to engage in its military undertaking in Vietnam.

IV. U.S. Intervention Violates the Constitution

The President has repeatedly stated and acknowledged that the United States is at war in Vietnam.[25] The Lawyers

[25] 52 DEP'T STATE BULL. 606, 838 (1965). Arthur Krock, "By Any Other Name, It's Still War," The New York Times, June 10, 1965.

Committee on American Policy Towards Vietnam in its memorandum of law took the position that our intervention is violative of our own Constitution. The Committee predicated its conclusion on the provisions of Article 1, Section 8, clause 11, in which the power to declare war is confided exclusively to the Congress. Congress alone can make that solemn commitment. The clause granting this power does not read "on the recommendation of the President" or that the "President with the advice and consent of Congress may declare war." As former Assistant Secretary of State James Grafton Rogers has observed, "The omission is significant. There was to be no war unless Congress took the initiative."[26]

The Supreme Court has held that

> Nothing in our Constitution is plainer than that declaration of war is entrusted only to Congress. . . . With all its defects, delays, and inconveniences, men have discovered no technique for long preserving free government except that the executive be under the law, and that the law be made by parliamentary deliberation.[27]

President Woodrow Wilson underscored the President's lack of power to declare war in his historic statement to a joint session of Congress on April 2, 1917:

> I have called the Congress into extraordinary session because there are serious, very serious, choices of policy to be made, and made immediately, which it was neither right nor constitutionally permissible that I should assume the responsibility of making.

---

[26] ROGERS, WORLD POLICING AND THE CONSTITUTION 21 (1945).

[27] *Youngstown Sheet & Tube Company* v. *Sawyer,* 343 U.S. 579, 642, 655 (1952) (Jackson, J.).

Congress has not declared war in Vietnam and the President does not claim that any declaration of war supports his actions in Vietnam. In fact, the President has been reported to be extremely reluctant to ask Congress to declare war.[28]

The writer of the "legality position" article, however, takes the position that the Southeast Asia Resolution (Tonkin Resolution) of August 10, 1964, is "undoubtedly the clearest and most unequivocal Congressional sanction of the President's deployment of United States forces for the defense of South Vietnam." The writer then quotes Senators John Sherman Cooper, J. William Fulbright, and Wayne Morse during the debates on the Tonkin Resolution, and he concludes that since "the resolution authorizes the President 'to make war,' it surely has the same legal effect as a Congressional 'declaration of war' *in haec verba* would have had."

It would seem that the action of Congress under the conditions that prevailed when the Tonkin Resolution was submitted constitutes, at most, an ultimatum and not a declaration of war.

Senator Fulbright in a recent article stated:

> The joint resolution was a blank check signed by the Congress in an atmosphere of urgency that seemed at the time to preclude debate. . . .
>
> I myself, as chairman of the Foreign Relations Committee, served as floor manager of the Southeast Asia resolution and did all I could to bring about its prompt and overwhelming adoption. I did so because I was confident that President Johnson would use our endorsement with wisdom and restraint. I was also influenced by partisanship: an election campaign was in progress and I had no wish to

[28] The Wall Street Journal, "The U.S. May Become More Candid on Rising Land-War Involvement," June 17, 1965, page 1.

> make any difficulties for the President in his race against a Republican candidate whose election I thought would be a disaster for the country. My role in the adoption of the resolution of Aug. 7, 1964, is a source of neither pleasure nor pride to me today.[29]

There have been instances when the President has sent United States forces abroad without a declaration of war by Congress. These have ranged from minor engagements between pirates and American ships on the high seas to the dispatch of our armed forces to Latin American countries and our involvement in Korea. But, except for the Korean war, none of these instances remotely involved so massive and dangerous a military undertaking as the war in Vietnam. And in the Korean war the United States fought under the aegis of the United Nations.

Since Mr. Deutsch assumes that the Tonkin Resolution does constitute a "Congressional declaration of war *in haec verba*," empowering the President to act, it is fitting to recall that on May 6, 1954, at a time when the fall of Dienbienphu was imminent, then Senator Lyndon B. Johnson criticized the President in these terms:

> We will insist upon clear explanations of the policies in which we are asked to cooperate. We will insist that we and the American people be treated as adults—that we have the facts without sugar coating.
>
> The function of Congress is not simply to appropriate money and leave the problem of national security at that.[30]

---

[29] The New York Times Magazine, "The Fatal Arrogance of Power," May 15, 1966, page 28. This article was based on an address at the Johns Hopkins School of Advanced Studies.

[30] Jackson, The Role and Problems of Congress with Reference to Atomic War, Publication No. L 54–135, Industrial College of the Armed Forces (1954).

Congress should, therefore, exercise its constitutional responsibility as a coequal branch of government of checks and balances to determine whether this country shall continue to be involved in the war in Vietnam. Under the rule of law, compliance with the forms and procedures of law are as imperative as compliance with the substance of law.

What Action to Take in This Solemn Hour

This is a solemn hour in history. We have a moral obligation to history to return to the high purposes and principles of the United Nations. We may be on the threshold of a further involvement in Asia. The United Nations Charter forbids our unilateral intervention in the circumstances which exist in Vietnam.

It may be that the world could be brought closer to peace if we agreed to the following:

1. Declaration of a six months' (or more) cease-fire to create conditions for negotiations.

2. That during the cease-fire period the Soviet Union and Great Britain (the co-chairmen of the Geneva Conference in 1954) be requested to reconvene the 1954 Conference and invite all the nations which participated at the "Final Declaration" of the Geneva Conference on July 21, 1954, to renegotiate the 1954 Accord.

3. If efforts to negotiate prove inconclusive, we should resort to the candor urged by an eminent political scientist. Emmet John Hughes, after a recent searching visit to Vietnam, details his views of the conditions in that country and concludes his report as follows:

> . . . And it means the wisdom to sense that American repute in Asia is not dignified but diminished by untiring

war for the unattainable victory . . . and American honor is not tarnished but brightened when so great a power can say, with quiet assurance: we have judged poorly, fought splendidly, and survive confidently.

I can think of no other way that the leaders of the United States might match the courage of the soldiers they have dispatched.[31]

---

[31] Newsweek, May 30, 1966, pages 22–23.

APPENDIX B:

The U.S. Quarantine of Cuba and the Rule of Law*

It may well be that when future historians evaluate the twentieth century, commencing with the signing of the United Nations Charter in 1945, they will find that the confrontation of the United States and the Union of Soviet Socialist Republics in 1962 during the Cuban quarantine proved to be the turning point in the history of the Atomic Age.

In the February 1963 issue of the *American Bar Association Journal* Eustace Seligman, a distinguished member of the New York Bar, in an article entitled "The Legality of the U.S. Quarantine Action Under the United Nations Charter," posed this question: "Was our action in imposing the quarantine of this nature in violation of our written word?" That author's answer was that it was *not*.

It is this writer's view that the United States quarantine action was not only in violation of our written word, as found in the Act of Chapultepec, the United Nations Charter, the Rio Pact, the Bogotá Charter, and the Caracas Dec-

* Reprinted from the *American Bar Association Journal*, August 1963.

laration, but also that it was in violation of international law.

Mr. Seligman based his position on provisions of the United Nations Charter, the doctrine of self-defense, and the action of the Organization of American States. I shall deal seriatim with the views urged in support of the "legality" position.

The United Nations Charter is the first multinational treaty since the League of Nations under which nations, large and small, united to maintain peace. The organization, basing itself "on the principle of the sovereign equality of all its members," agreed to "settle their international disputes by peaceful means" and "to refrain in their international relations from the threat of use of force against the territorial integrity or political independence of any state." [1]

The nations that were united under the charter in 1945 do, however, maintain different political and economic systems. If world peace is to be attained by a submission to the rule of law, it will also become obligatory for the conflicting political and economic systems to understand each other and not to resort to the use of force whenever there arise differences that are not readily soluble.

The enormity of President Kennedy's action in declaring the quarantine of Cuba was commented on soon after it was taken by Henry W. Edgerton, a judge of the United States Court of Appeals for the District of Columbia Circuit and a distinguished American jurist, in a letter published in the *New York Times* on November 14, 1962:

> Many people think events have justified President Kennedy's toughness in the Cuban crisis. This is a little like

---

[1] U.N. CHARTER art. 2, paras. 3–4.

thinking that if a man plays "Russian roulette" and escapes death, the event proves that the act was reasonable. The great differences between the two cases are obvious. On the one hand, the President sought to promote the public good. On the other hand, he risked many millions of lives besides his own.

Removal of Cuban bases does not make us safe. We were unsafe before they were there and shall still be unsafe when they are gone.

Organization, Background and Role of the O.A.S.

After the outbreak of World War II and when in 1940 it appeared that the United States might become involved, the foreign ministers of the Latin American countries met.[2] The need for political cooperation between the states in the Western Hemisphere became more urgent. The influence of the Axis sympathizers in some Latin American countries became more apparent. But the dominant forces in the chancellories of the American states subscribed to the concept that "an attack on one is an attack on all." Brazil and Mexico became active belligerents in World War II.

The organization conference of the United Nations at San Francisco had been preceded by the Mexico City Conference on Problems of Peace and War in March 1945. This conference afforded the Latin American countries the opportunity to express their views and apprehensions regarding the security they would receive under the Dumbarton Oaks proposals of the Big Four, which had been released immediately prior to the San Francisco Conference. At the end of the Mexico City Conference, the Act of Chapultepec

---

[2] Second Meeting of Consultation of the Ministers of Foreign Affairs of the American Republics, Havana, July 20–30, 1940.

was adopted. This act adopted the following definition of aggression:

> That every attack of a state against the integrity or the inviolability of the territory, or against the sovereignty or political independence of an American state, shall, conformably to Part III hereof, be considered as an act of aggression against the other states which sign this act.[3]

After the United Nations Charter was signed, the South American republics met at Rio de Janeiro in 1947 to consider a "regional arrangement" under Chapter VIII of the United Nations Charter. The Inter-American Treaty of Reciprocal Assistance, often referred to as the Rio Pact, was adopted. This pact merely fixed the principles that were to govern the inter-American community when its security is threatened. The Charter of the Organization of American States, which was adopted at Bogotá in 1948, reaffirmed the principle that all undertakings on the part of the American states require congruity with the United Nations Charter.

Because the use of armed force is implicit in the declaration issued by President Kennedy on October 23, 1962, imposing the Cuban quarantine, it seems appropriate to quote Sections 15 and 16 of the Charter of the Organization of American States:

> Article 15. No state or group of states has the right to intervene, directly or indirectly, for any reason whatever, in the internal or external affairs of any other state. The foregoing principle prohibits not only armed force but also any other form of interference or attempted threat against the

---

[3] For a full discussion of the United Nations and the inter-American system, see *The Inter-American Security System and the Cuban Crisis* 9–14 (The Association of the Bar of the City of New York, 1962).

> personality of the state or against its political, economic, and cultural elements.
>
> Article 16. No state may use or encourage the use of coercive measures of an economic or political character in order to force the sovereign will of another state and obtain from it advantages of any kind.

A literal reading of these articles reveals the sweeping character of the pact. "Taking them together, they seem to denounce collective, as well as individual, pressures exerted by one state on another, even with regard to the external affairs which affront the security of other states." [4]

Legal Aspects of the Cuban Confrontation

The writer agrees with Mr. Seligman that as a nation that professes to believe in the sanctity of obligations, we must be bound not only with the observance of all treaties, charters, and pacts, but with the "legal niceties" as well. Therefore, I will consider the applicable doctrine of international law as well as our obligations under the United Nations Charter and the pacts and declarations that the United States has been a party to during recent decades.

1. Aspects of Legality Under the Rio Pact and Bogotá Charter

Before discussing the legal implications of the quarantine of Cuba under the Charter of the Organization of American States, it is desirable to advert briefly to the Punta del Este meeting of January 22, 1962, which was convened pursuant to the Treaty of Reciprocal Assistance. This was signed at

---

[4] *Id.* at 17 and 37.

Rio de Janeiro in 1947 and is often referred to as the cornerstone of the inter-American regional security system.

The Punta del Este conference was called because of the need for meeting the challenge of the revolution in Cuba. The United States stopped buying Cuban sugar, asserted in behalf of its nationals the observance of their property rights, and ultimately completely severed relations with Cuba in 1961. The Bay of Pigs invasion failed, and Cuba moved closer to the Soviet Union. Finally, Castro declared his attachment to Marxism-Leninism, and the gauntlet was thrown down.

These events posed the following questions:

1. What would be the effect of an invitation to a Communist country by a Western Hemisphere country?

2. Under the United Nations Charter, could the United States use force unilaterally to assert its interest under the Monroe Doctrine and oppose such invitation?

3. If the United States could not act unilaterally under the Monroe Doctrine, could the O.A.S. under the Caracas Declaration or the Rio Pact take action to bar an invitation to a Communist country?

4. If action were taken by the O.A.S. against a member country, would that constitute a "coercive measure of an economic or political character" which would constitute a direct or indirect intervention "in the internal or external affairs of any other state"?

The Punta del Este conference considered these and other questions raised by the new developments in Cuba. No specific charges against Cuba were made, but inquiries into "the threats to the peace and to the political independence of the American states that might arise from the intervention of extracontinental powers directed toward breaking

American solidarity"[5] were the basis for the call for the conference.

General-good and welfare resolutions were adopted, including a reiteration of the principles of nonintervention and self-determination and the holding of free elections. But the basic resolution adopted was the one calling for exclusion of the existing Cuban Government from participation in the inter-American system. "The opponents of exclusion argued insistently that, in view of the absence of any provision in the charter (Bogotá, 1948) fixing the terms of exclusion, the exclusion of a member state from the organization could not be effected without an amendment to the charter, which would require the calling of a special conference and ratification by a two-thirds vote, after which another conference would be required to complete the exclusion."[6]

The charter contains no provision for suspension or exclusion of a member state from the right of membership. The Covenant of the League of Nations had an express provision for exclusion (Article 16) and the United Nations Charter (Article 6) also provides for the manner of expulsion of a member.

The query really posed, therefore, is whether under the Rio Pact and the Bogotá Charter, which in essence constitute a multilateral treaty comparable to the League of Nations and the United Nations, a member country can be excluded without an amendment of the charter, when the existing charter makes no such provision.[7]

In considering the legality of the Cuban quarantine, students of international law must first determine whether

---

[5] 56 AM. J. INT'L L. 470 (1962).
[6] *Id.* at 473.
[7] *Id.* at 474.

Cuba could be deprived of its rights under the charter to be immune from intervention in her internal or external affairs by the use of economic coercive measures by the simple stratagem of exclusion from participation in the inter-American system, particularly when the exclusion may have been in violation of the charter. Had Cuba not been excluded from membership in the O.A.S., she could have pleaded her immunity from quarantine under Articles 15 and 16 of the Bogotá Charter. Exclusion of Cuba, it would seem therefore, could have been possible only after an amendment of the charter.[8]

2. *Aspects of Legality Under International Law*

(a) Doctrine of the "Freedom of the Seas."

Another query which students of international law must answer is whether President Kennedy's quarantine proclamation is legal under the time-honored doctrine of freedom of the high seas. The pre-emption of vast sections of the Pacific by the United States, Great Britain, and the U.S.S.R. during their nuclear bomb testings was the first rejection by major maritime powers of the freedom of the seas doctrine. Are we to assume that the cold war has completely rejected this doctrine?

The freedom of the high seas doctrine has over a period of more than 300 years become the keystone of international law. The law of the seas has often been referred to as the earliest international law. The United States Supreme Court has held that "upon the ocean in time of peace, all possess entire equality. It is the common highway of all, appropri-

[8] While the resolution of exclusion adopted at Punta del Este was directed against the *government* of Cuba as distinguished from the *state,* the fact is that the quarantine imposed sanctions on the state of Cuba.

ated to the use of all, and no one can vindicate to himself a superior or exclusive prerogative there." [9]

A leading French scholar has declared: "The high sea does not form a part of the territory of any state. No state can have over it a right of ownership, sovereignty or jurisdiction. None can lawfully claim to dictate laws for the high seas." [10]

C. John Colombos, a distinguished scholar, wrote:

> Today it is universally recognized that the open sea is not susceptible of appropriation and that no state can obtain such possession of it as would legally be necessary to give rise to a claim of property. The high sea cannot be subject to a right of sovereignty for it is the necessary means of communication between nations and its free use thus constitutes an indispensable element for international trade and navigation. . . . *It follows that no given state is entitled to occupy it or to prescribe its use to other states.* [Emphasis added.] [11]

In his memoirs Anthony Eden discusses the diplomatic exchange between the United States and Great Britain during the Guatemala episode of 1954. He refers to Secretary of State Dulles's order "to establish what amounted to a blockade of the Guatemala coast." The order directed that "any suspicious vessels were to be searched for arms, with the permission of the governments concerned, if there was time to obtain it." Eden, then Foreign Secretary, asserted that "We could not possibly acquiesce in forcible action against British ships on the high seas. The rule of law still obtained in this country, and it was of great importance to

[9] *The Mariana Flora,* 24 U.S. 1, 42 (1826), Story, J.

[10] 1 Fauchille, Traite de Droit International Public 11 (1923–1926).

[11] Colombos, International Law of the Sea 39–40 (1954).

us as a maritime nation that it should also obtain on the high seas."

Mr. Eden writes that despite this representation, Mr. Dulles still did not exclude the possibility of the United States Navy's taking action against British ships without Britain's permission. He (Dulles) went on to remark that "in the cold war conditions of today, the rules applicable in the past no longer seemed to him to meet the situation and required to be revised or flexibly applied." [12]

But the United States also violated its written word, when the Cuban quarantine was declared, because of its commitment of April 29, 1958, at Geneva, when it signed the Convention of the High Seas. Article 2 of that convention reads:

> The high seas being open to all nations, no state may validly purport to subject any part of them to its sovereignty. Freedom of the high seas is exercised under the conditions laid down by these articles and by the other rules of international law. It comprises *inter alia,* both for coastal and noncoastal states:
>
> (1) Freedom of navigation;
> (2) Freedom of fishing;
> (3) Freedom to lay submarine cables and pipelines;
> (4) Freedom to fly over the high seas.
>
> These freedoms, and others which are recognized by the general principles of international law, shall be exercised by all states with reasonable regard to the interests of other states in their exercise of the freedom of the high seas.[13]

(b) Doctrine of Self-Preservation or Self-Defense.

President Kennedy in his October 22, 1962, address to

---

[12] FULL CIRCLE, THE MEMOIRS OF ANTHONY EDEN 151–152 (1960).
[13] 52 AM. J. INT'L L. 842–843 (1958).

the people of the United States stated that in declaring the quarantine of Cuba he was "acting, therefore, in defense of our own security and of the entire Western Hemisphere." If it is assumed that Soviet missiles in Cuba were actually a threat to the United States, the question is whether that threat was of such a nature that a blockade of Cuba was justified under the doctrine known in international law as the principle of self-preservation or self-defense.

Mr. Seligman in his "legality" article gives an example of the exercise of the right of anticipatory self-defense by referring to the British seizure of the Danish fleet after the Peace of Tilsit in 1807. He points out that the British were fearful at that time that the Danish fleet would fall into the hands of the French and that the fleet would be used against the British. Judge Hersh Lauterpacht is quoted to the effect that while the action by Great Britain in that situation was condemned by most Continental writers, it was approved by many British and American writers.

Since Mr. Seligman gives this episode as an example of the permissible use of anticipatory self-defense, I will advert to a more recent example of a contrary view on the use of anticipatory self-defense.

Bin Cheng, in his treatise *General Principles of Law as Applied by International Courts and Tribunals,* reviews an example of anticipatory self-defense that was rejected by the International Military Tribunal:

> One of the legal problems which arose at the time of "German Major War Criminals" (1945–1946) was whether or not the taking of preventive measures in a neutral country is permissible when it is certain that the neutral is on the point of being, but is not yet, invaded by the enemy. The question arose in connection with the German invasion of Norway launched on April 9, 1940, for which

> the defendant Erich Raeder was charged with criminal responsibility.
>
> Counsel for the defendant invoked "the right of self-defense," and argued that the object of the German invasion was to forstall an imminent British invasion of Norway.[14]

The International Military Tribunal in its judgment in the *German Major War Criminals Case* (1946) held, in part:

> When the [German] plans for an attack on Norway were being made, they were not made for the purpose of forestalling an imminent Allied landing, but, at the most, that they might prevent an Allied occupation at some future date.[15]

Further, the Court held:

> It must be remembered that preventive action in foreign territory is justified only in case of "an instant and overwhelming necessity for self-defense, leaving no choice of means, and no moment of deliberation." (*The Caroline Case,* Moore's *Digest of International Law,* II, 412.) [16]

The words "an instant and overwhelming necessity for self-defense, *leaving no choice of means, and no moment of deliberation*" [emphasis added] are from the well-known Caroline Case, in which reference is made to a formulation of the doctrine of self-defense by Secretary of State Daniel

---

[14] Bin Cheng, General Principles of Law as Applied by International Courts and Tribunals 88–89 (1953).

[15] *Id.* at 89. See also, International Military Tribunal, Nuremberg, German Major War Criminals Case 171, 207 (1946).

[16] Bin Cheng, *op. cit. supra* note 14, at 84.

Webster. The Caroline Case arose during the Canadian Rebellion of 1837. In 1842 during an exchange between our State Department and the British Plenipotentiary Ashburton, Webster defined the conditions under which anticipatory self-defense is permissible, and this formulation was relied on by the International Military Tribunal when it rendered its decision at Nuremberg.

When the Cuban quarantine declaration was issued, it is fair to assume that the convening of the Security Council of the United Nations would have afforded "moments of deliberation" and resulted in a "choice of means." The fact that the confrontation was ultimately resolved is some indication that it could have been solved without the military confrontation that was employed.

What is particularly ominous is that a precedent may have been set for the unilateral resort to the doctrine of self-defense. In the view of one authority, anticipatory self-defense "is another 'unruly horse' that presents the difficulty of where you will be carried if you mount. Pushed to an extreme anticipatory self-defense is aggression." [17]

3. Aspects of Legality Under the United Nations Charter

The presence of offensive missile bases anywhere in the world is a grave threat to all nations. During the Security Council debate on the issue of the validity of the Cuban quarantine, Adlai E. Stevenson replied to the Soviet delegate as follows:

> One other point I should like to make is to invite attention to the casual remark of the Soviet representative claiming that we have thirty-five bases in foreign countries.

---

[17] Brochure, *op. cit. supra* note 3, at 34.

> The fact is that there are missiles comparable to those being placed in Cuba with the forces of only those of our allies. They were established there only by a decision of the heads of governments, meeting in December, 1957, which was compelled to authorize such arrangements by virtue of a prior Soviet decision to introduce its own missiles capable of destroying the countries of Western Europe.[18]

The United Nations Charter provision relative to the quarantine of Cuba is Article 2, paragraph 4, which provides:

> All members shall refrain in their international relations from the threat or use of force against the territorial integrity or political independence of any member or state, or in any other manner inconsistent with the purposes of the United Nations.

Arthur Larson, director of the World Rule of Law Institute at Duke University, urged in a letter published in the *New York Times* on November 12, 1962, that "Since the quarantine was not aimed at the 'territorial integrity' or 'political independence' of Cuba, the question is whether it was in any way inconsistent with the purposes of the United Nations."

The Cuban quarantine issue, it would seem, pivots rather on Article 51 of the United Nations Charter, and less on the doctrine of self-defense or self-preservation in international law. The first sentence of this article provides that:

> Nothing in the present charter shall impair the inherent right of individual or collective self-defense, if *an armed*

---

[18] U.N. Doc. No. S/PV 1025, page 62.

> *attack* occurs against a member of the organization, until the Security Council has taken the measures necessary to maintain international peace and security. [Emphasis added.]

Since the presence of long-range missiles cannot be considered an armed attack, the quarantine declaration, made before the Security Council could convene, constituted an act in violation of Article 51. Nor could the anticipatory self-defense doctrine in international law be relied on as justification for the act of quarantine, in light of the discussion of that doctrine in the Caroline Case and the judgment of the International Military Tribunal mentioned above.

Professor Philip C. Jessup, the United States jurist at present serving on the International Court of Justice, in interpreting Article 51 states:

> A case could be made out for self-defense under the traditional law where the injury was threatened but no attack had yet taken place. Under the charter, alarming military preparations by a neighboring state could justify resort to the Security Council, but would not justify resort to *anticipatory force* by the state which believed itself threatened. [Emphasis added.] [19]

Whereas under international law prior to the adoption of the United Nations Charter the invocation of self-defense was left to a subjective determination by the state which believed itself threatened, Article 51 sets out an objective condition—"an armed attack"—as the only basis for self-defense.

One writer concludes that "henceforth the threat of attack

---

[19] JESSUP, A MODERN LAW OF NATIONS 166 (1947).

would not sanction anticipatory force by the adversary." [20]

Judge Lauterpacht, considering the principle of self-preservation in international law since the signing of the United Nations Charter, states: "Thus the Charter of the United Nations leaves intact the inherent right of individual or collective self-defense in case of *armed attack* against a member of the United Nations until the Security Council takes action." [Emphasis added.] [21]

The use of unilateral force in self-defense of the kind projected in the Cuban quarantine may constitute "preventive war." If it should set a precedent, then any member of the United Nations could resort to this measure whenever, in its opinion, nuclear missiles on its border became a threat to its security.

The attempt to quarantine Guatemala was explained in 1954 on the theory that, according to Mr. Dulles, "cold war conditions rule out the traditional safeguard of international law." The Cuban quarantine is being justified on the theory that offensive nuclear weapons ninety miles from the United States constitute a threat to the security of the United States and the Western Hemisphere.

A fortnight after President Kennedy declared the Cuban quarantine, Judge Edgerton, in his letter to the *New York Times* quoted above, concluded with the following recommendation:

> Since nuclear knowledge cannot be unlearned or prevented from spreading, we cannot long survive without universal disarmament and world government. We can

---

[20] Joseph H. Crown, letter to *New York Times,* November 26, 1962. See also, 18 U.S.C. §960.

[21] 1 OPPENHEIM, INTERNATIONAL LAW 267 (rev. by Lauterpacht, 8th ed., 1955–1957). See also, LAUTERPACHT, THE DEVELOPMENT OF INTERNATIONAL LAW BY THE INTERNATIONAL COURT 316–317 (1958).

take some unilateral steps toward peace, such as dismantling our Turkish bases, withdrawing from Southeast Asia and ceasing to make nuclear tests. But the most important step toward peace that we can take is a change of attitude.

The need is urgent to move away from international hatred and toward international tolerance.

APPENDIX C:

Lawyers Committee on American Policy Towards Vietnam

WILLIAM L. STANDARD Chairman.
CAREY MC WILLIAMS Vice-Chairman.
JOSEPH H. CROWN Secretary-Treasurer.
ROBERT L. BOEHM Chairman, Executive Board.
WILLIAM MEYERS Director of Organizational Activities.

Consultative Council:

RICHARD A. FALK *Chairman.* Milbank Professor of International Law, Princeton University.

RICHARD J. BARNET Co-Director, Institute for Policy Studies, Washington, D.C.

JOHN H. E. FRIED Professor of Political Science, City University of N.Y. (City College).

JOHN H. HERZ Professor of International Relations, City University of N.Y. (City College).

STANLEY HOFFMANN Professor of Government and International Law, Harvard University.

WALLACE MC CLURE Lecturer on International Law, Universities of Virginia, Duke, Dacca, Karachi.

SAUL H. MENDLOVITZ Professor of International Law, Rutgers University School of Law.

RICHARD S. MILLER Professor of International Law, Ohio State University College of Law.

HANS J. MORGENTHAU Albert A. Michelson Distinguished Service Professor of Political Science and Modern History, University of Chicago.

WILLIAM G. RICE Professor of International Law, University of Wisconsin Law School.

BURNS H. WESTON Professor of International Law, University of Iowa, College of Law.

QUINCY WRIGHT Professor Emeritus of International Law, University of Chicago.

APPENDIX D:

The "Nuremberg Principles of International Law"

Unanimously affirmed by the General Assembly of the United Nations on December 11, 1946, as formulated by the International Law Commission, June–July 1950.

Principle I

Any person who commits an act which constitutes a crime under international law is responsible therefor and liable to punishment.

Principle II

The fact that internal law does not impose a penalty for an act which constitutes a crime under international law does not relieve the person who committed the act from responsibility under international law.

Principle III

The fact that a person who committed an act which constitutes a crime under international law acted as Head of

State or responsible government official does not relieve him from responsibility under international law.

Principle IV

The fact that a person acted pursuant to order of his Government or of a superior does not relieve him from responsibility under international law, provided a moral choice was in fact possible to him.

Principle V

Any person charged with a crime under international law has the right to a fair trial on the facts and law.

Principle VI

The crimes hereinafter set out are punishable as crimes under international law:

a. Crimes against peace:

(i) Planning, preparation, initiation or waging of a war of aggression or a war in violation of international treaties, agreements or assurances;

(ii) Participation in a common plan or conspiracy for the accomplishment of any of the acts mentioned under (i).

b. War crimes:

Violations of the laws or customs of war which include, but are not limited to, murder, ill-treatment or deportation to slave-labour or for any other purpose of civilian population of or in occupied territory, murder or ill-treatment of prisoners of war or persons on the seas, killing of hostages, plunder of public or private property, wanton destruction of cities, towns, or villages, or devastation not justified by military necessity.

c. Crimes against humanity:

Murder, extermination, enslavement, deportation and

other inhuman acts done against any civilian population, or persecutions on political, racial or religious grounds, when such acts are done or such persecutions are carried on in execution of or in connection with any crime against peace or any war crime.

Principle VII

Complicity in the commission of a crime against peace, a war crime, or a crime against humanity as set forth in Principle VI is a crime under international law.

NOTES

Chapter 1: *The New Colonialism*

1. *Guardian,* Nov. 29, 1969, p. 11 (based upon U.S. Government statistics on Vietnam casualties).

Chapter 2: *The Escalation of Resistance*

1. "The Student Revolt Against Liberalism," *Annals of the American Academy of Political and Social Sciences,* March 1969, p. 86.
2. "Student Attitudes and Concerns," *Columbia Forum,* Winter 1968, XI, 4, 42–43.
3. *New York Times,* April 23, 1969.
4. *New York Times,* May 23, 1969.
5. McKinney's Consolidated Laws of New York, Civil Rights Law, Book 8, p. 22.
6. CBS News, official transcript of CBS Radio Network Broadcast, April 27, 1969, pp. 19–20.
7. *New York Times,* April 26, 1969.
8. *New York Times,* May 24, 1969.
9. *New York Times,* June 3, 1969.
10. *New York Times,* June 3, 1969.
11. *New York Times,* June 10, 1969.

Chapter 3: *Policeman of the World*

1. 1947 U.S. Code Cong. Serv., pp. 1811, 1813. Henry Steele Commager, Ed., *Documents of American History* (New York: Appleton), I, 524–526.
2. D. F. Fleming, *The Cold War and Its Origins, 1950–1960* (Garden City: Doubleday, 1961), II, 602.
3. *Congressional Record,* July 27, 1953, p. 9853. Ronald J. Caridi, *The Korean War and American Politics* (Philadelphia: University of Pennsylvania Press, 1968), p. 275.
4. *The Truth About Vietnam* (San Diego: Greenleaf Classics, 1966), p. 170.
5. J. T. Adams, Ed., *Dictionary of American History* (New York: Charles Scribner's Sons), Vol. 6.
6. Anthony Eden, *Full Circle* (Boston: Houghton Mifflin, 1960), pp. 151–2.
7. Quincy Wright, "United States Intervention in Lebanon," *American Journal of International Law,* Jan. 1959, pp. 112, 115.
8. Eduardo Galiano, *Guatemala: Occupied Country* (New York: Monthly Review Press, 1969), pp. 52–53.
9. Carl Oglesby, "Trapped in a System." Included in a pamphlet published by the Campus Vietnam Day Committee, Berkeley Free Press, February 7, 1966.
10. Business Executives Move for Vietnam Peace, *Washington Watch,* No. 52, May 12, 1969.
11. *The Truth About Vietnam, op. cit.,* p. 365.
12. *Ibid.,* p. 365.

Chapter 4: *The Background for Our Involvement in Vietnam*

1. Edgar Snow, *The Other Side of the River* (New York: Random House, 1962), p. 686. *Congressional Record,* May 9, 1967.
2. *The Truth About Vietnam* (San Diego: Greenleaf Classics, 1966), p. 28.

3. Anthony Eden, *Full Circle* (Boston: Houghton Mifflin, 1960), p. 121. Ashmore and Baggs, *Mission to Hanoi,* (New York: G. P. Putnam's Sons, 1968), p. 210.
4. Matthew B. Ridgway, *Korean War* (New York: Doubleday, 1967).

Chapter 5: *United States Intervention in Vietnam Is Illegal*

1. *Congressional Record,* March 10, 1966, 112, 5274–5279.
2. Kahin and Lewis, *The United States in Vietnam* (New York: Delta, 1967), p. 352.
3. *Ibid.,* pp. 367–376.
4. Dwight D. Eisenhower, *Mandate for Change: The White House Years, 1953–1956* (New York: Doubleday, 1963), p. 372.
5. Association d'Amitié Franco-Vietnamienne, *Chronology of the Vietnam War: Book I (1941–1966)* (Paris), p. 31.
6. Kahin and Lewis, *op. cit.,* p. 80.
7. *Dept. of State Bulletin,* Washington, D.C., March 7, 1966, p. 349.
8. *U.S. News & World Report,* Feb. 15, 1965, p. 64.
9. *Congressional Record,* March 10, 1966, 112, 5274–5279.
10. *101 Congressional Record,* 1955, pp. 1051–1052.
11. *112 Congressional Record,* 1966, p. 5558.
12. *101 Congressional Record,* 1955, pp. 1051–1052.
13. *The South East Asia Collective Defense Treaty,* 83rd Congress (Washington: U.S. Government Printing Office, 1954), pp. 28–29.
14. *Ibid,* p. 25.
15. *The Truth About Vietnam* (San Diego: Greenleaf Classics, 1966), p. 15.
16. *New York Times,* July 6, 1970.
17. Philip Jessup, *Modern Law of Nations* (New York: Macmillan, 1948), pp. 165–166.
18. Hans Kelsen, *The Law of the United Nations* (New York: Praeger, 1964).
19. Jessup, *op. cit.,* pp. 34–36.

20. *Congressional Record,* Senate, Jan. 24, 1966, p. 908.
21. *Ibid.*
22. *Congressional Record,* Senate, June 16, 1966, pp. 12856–12858.
23. *U.S. Chronicle,* 2, 22.
24. Lewis Henkin, *American Society of International Law Proceedings,* 1963, p. 148.
25. Edward S. Corwin, *The President: Office and Powers* (New York: New York University Press, 1957), p. 9.
26. *World Policing and the Constitution* (Boston: 1945), p. 21.
27. *Congressional Record,* June 9, 1965, p. 12528.
28. *The Truth About Vietnam, op. cit.,* p. 168.

Chapter 6: *Who Are the Aggressors?*

1. *United Nations General Assembly,* A/Ac. 134/5, April 7, 1969, p. 11.
2. *Dept. of State Bulletin,* Washington, D.C., Sept. 30, 1963, pp. 498–499.
3. "The War in Vietnam," *Congressional Record,* May 9, 1967, 113, 72, 4.
4. *Congressional Record,* Senate, May 9, 1967, 113, 72, 5.
5. *Ibid.,* p. 8.
6. Ashmore and Baggs, *Mission to Hanoi* (New York: G. P. Putnam's Sons, 1968), p. 258.
7. *Ibid.,* p. 276.
8. *I. F. Stone's Weekly,* Washington, D.C., Sept. 12, 1966.
9. Tom Wicker, "Lyndon Johnson vs. The Ghost of Jack Kennedy," *Esquire,* Nov. 1965, p. 87.
10. *Congressional Record,* Senate, May 9, 1967, 72, 10.
11. Anthony Austin, "Genesis of the Tonkin Resolution," *New York Times,* Aug. 27, 1967.

Chapter 7: *The Song My Massacre and United States War Crimes in Vietnam*

1. *Newsweek,* Dec. 8, 1969, p. 33–34.
2. *Ibid.,* pp. 33–34.

3. San Francisco *Chronicle,* Nov. 20, 1969.
4. *Newsweek,* Dec. 8, 1969, p. 33.
5. *Ibid.,* pp. 150–151.
6. *Newsweek,* Dec. 8, 1969, p. 33.
7. Noam Chomsky, *American Power and the New Mandarins.* (New York: Random House, 1969), p. 233.
8. Richard A. Falk, "War Crimes—The Circle of Responsibility," *The Nation,* Jan. 26, 1970, p. 79.
9. *Ibid.,* p. 77.
10. *Ibid.,* p. 81.
11. *Newsweek,* Dec. 8, 1969, p. 41.
12. *New York Times,* March 18, 1970, p. 1.
13. *Newsweek,* March 30, 1970, p. 20.
14. *O'Callahan v. Parker,* 395 U.S. 258, p. 265.
15. *New York Times,* April 5, 1970.
16. *Newsweek,* April 13, 1970, p. 30.

Chapter 8: *"Endless War" and the Military-Industrial Complex*

1. Richard W. Kaufman, "Unwarranted Influence of the Military-Industrial Complex," *New York Times Magazine,* June 22, 1969, p. 68.
2. *Ibid.*
3. *Ibid,* p. 72.
4. I. F. Stone, "The War Machine Under Nixon," *New York Review of Books,* Jan. 5, 1969, p. 6.
5. *Ibid.,* p. 6, footnote 5.
6. "Vietnam: Endless War," *Monthly Review,* April 1969, p. 9.

Chapter 9: *Total Withdrawal: The Only Solution*

1. James Reston, *New York Times,* Aug. 27, 1969.
2. *Newsweek,* Sept. 8, 1969, p. 17.
3. "Many GI's Disillusioned on War," *New York Times,* Aug. 4, 1969.
4. "Washington Dispatch," *Newsweek,* Aug. 11, 1969, p. 25.
5. *Ibid.*

6. *Washington Watch,* Sept. 4, 1969, No. 60, p. 3.
7. *New York Times,* dispatch from Bangkok, Thailand, Aug. 24, 1969.
8. Stewart Alsop, "Is the War Lost?" *Newsweek,* May 5, 1969.
9. *Guardian,* April 26, 1969, p. 12.
10. *The Truth About Vietnam* (San Diego: Greenleaf Classics, 1966), p. 167.
11. *Ibid.,* p. 175.
12. *Ibid.,* p. 197.
13. *Ibid.,* p. 193.
14. Clark Clifford, "A Viet Nam Reappraisal," *Foreign Affairs,* July 1969, pp. 617, 619.
15. *Ibid.,* p. 619.
16. *Ibid.*
17. *Ibid.,* pp. 621–622.
18. Clark Clifford, "Set a Date in Vietnam. Stick to It. Get Out," *Life,* May 22, 1970, p. 38.
19. *New York Times,* July 3, 1970.

Chapter 10: *The Cambodian Invasion: An Invitation to Disaster*

1. *Newsweek,* May 4, 1970, p. 21.
2. Clark Clifford, "Set a Date in Vietnam. Stick to It. Get Out," *Life,* May 22, 1970, p. 36.
3. Hugh Sidey, "Nixon in a Crisis of Leadership," *Life,* May 15, 1970, p. 28.
4. *New York Times,* May 1, 1970, p. 28.
5. "We the People," *New York Times,* June 11, 1970, p. 12.
6. Clifford, *op. cit.,* p. 34.
7. Wilfred Burchett, "The U.S. Cannot Win in Cambodia," *Guardian,* June 6, 1970, p. 10.
8. *Newsweek,* March 30, 1970, p. 20.
9. Clifford, *op. cit.,* p. 36.
10. Henry Steele Commager, Ed., *Documents of American History* (New York: Appleton), I, 524–526.

11. Noam Chomsky, "Cambodia," *New York Review of Books,* June 4, 1970, p. 39.
12. D. F. Fleming, *The Cold War and Its Origins* (New York: Doubleday, 1961), 1, 597–599.
13. Arthur Schlesinger, Jr., *New York Times,* November 17, 1968, p. 47.
14. *Ibid.*
15. *The Truth About Vietnam* (San Diego: Greenleaf Classics, 1966), pp. 239–240.
16. *Ibid.,* p. 333.
17. *Newsweek,* May 30, 1966, pp. 22–23.
18. *New York Times,* October 17, 1969.
19. "Indochina War Is Stirring Dissension on a Widening Scale Within the Ranks of the Army," *New York Times,* June 21, 1970, p. 1.
20. *Ibid.,* p. 1.
21. *Newsweek,* June 15, 1970, p. 72.
22. *Monthly Review,* June 1970, p. 8.

Chapter 11: *A Dunkirk, a Dienbienphu, or a Hiroshima*

1. Clark Clifford, "Set a Date in Vietnam. Stick to It. Get Out," *Life,* May 22, 1970, p. 36.
2. Editorial, *The Nation,* January 12, 1970.
3. *New York Times,* June 8, 1970, pp. 1, 3.
4. *Congressional Record,* June 11, 1970, p. S8828.
5. "Indochina Debate in Senate Shifts to Mercenary Issues," *New York Times,* June 13, 1970.
6. Noam Chomsky, *New York Review of Books,* June 4, 1970, p. 39.
7. *New York Times,* June 14, 1970, p. 114.
8. Richard Barnet, "Use of Nuclear Weapons in Indo-China" (speech read on May 23, 1970, at Toronto, Canada, before the Multi-National Lawyers Conference on Vietnam, Laos, and Cambodia).
9. *Monthly Review,* June 1970, p. 8 (footnote).
10. Richard Barnet, "Will the President Use Nuclear Weapons?" (address available through "Business Executives

Move for Vietnam Peace," 901 Worth Howard Street, Baltimore, Md. 21201).

11. Richard Barnet, "Use of Nuclear Weapons in Indo-China" (address available through Lawyers Committee on American Policy Towards Vietnam, 38 Park Row, New York, N.Y. 10038).

READING LIST

Adams, J. T., ed., *Dictionary of American History*. New York: Charles Scribner's Sons. Vol. VI.

Ashmore and Baggs, *Mission to Hanoi*. New York: G. P. Putnam's Sons, 1968.

Association d'Amitié Franco-Vietnamienne, *Chronology of the Vietnam War: Book I (1941–1966)*. Paris.

Caridi, Robert J., *The Korean War and American Politics*. Philadelphia: University of Pennsylvania Press, 1968.

Chomsky, Noam, *American Power and the New Mandarins*. New York: Random House, 1969.

Commager, Henry Steele, ed., *Documents of American History*. New York: Appleton, Vol. I.

Corwin, Edward S., *The President: Office and Powers*. New York: New York University Press, 1957.

Eden, Anthony, *Full Circle*. Boston: Houghton Mifflin, 1960.

Eisenhower, Dwight D., *Mandate for Change: The White House Years, 1953–1956*. New York: Doubleday, 1963.

Fleming, D. F., *The Cold War and Its Origins, 1950–1960*. Garden City: Doubleday, 1961. Vol. II.

Galiano, Edwardo, *Guatemala: Occupied Country*. New York: Monthly Review Press, 1969.

Jessup, Philip, *Modern Law of Nations*. New York: MacMillan, 1948.

Kahin and Lewis, *The United States in Vietnam*. New York: Delta, 1967.

Kelsen, Hans, *The Law of the United Nations.* New York: Praeger, 1964.

Ridgway, Matthew B., *Korean War.* New York: Doubleday, 1967.

Snow, Edgar, *The Other Side of the River.* New York: Random House, 1962.

INDEX

About the Author

WILLIAM L. STANDARD is an alumnus of Columbia College and the New York University School of Law. He was admitted to practice in the State of New York in 1926 and admitted to practice in the United States Supreme Court in 1938. He has argued appeals in that Court and in each of the United States Courts of Appeal for the Second, Third, Fourth, and Fifth Circuits.

Mr. Standard has served as chairman of the Lawyers Committee on American Policy Towards Vietnam since its organization in 1965. He is a member of the American Branch of the International Law Association, a senior member of the Inter-American Bar Association, and past chairman of the Maritime Law Section of that association. He has been chairman of the Constitutional Law Committee and a national officer of the National Lawyers Guild. He is also a member of the Maritime Law Association of the United States and a former chairman of the Committee on Admiralty of the New York County Lawyers Association. He was general counsel to the National Maritime Union of America (C.I.O.) from 1937 to 1948. Mr. Standard is senior partner of the law firm of Standard, Weisberg, Heckerling & Rosow, in New York.

He has contributed articles on international law, international conventions, and maritime law to the *American Bar Association Journal; Inter-American Law Review* (Tulane University); *Law in the Service of Peace;* the International Association of Democratic Lawyers Review (Brussels, Belgium); and the *New Jersey Bar Journal,* as well as local bar association publications.